Final Environmental Assessment
for FutureFuel Chemical Company
Electric Drive Vehicle Battery
and Component Manufacturing Initiative Project
Batesville, AR

August 2010

Prepared for:
Department of Energy
National Energy Technology Laboratory

Electric Drive Vehicle Battery and
Component Manufacturing Initiative Project
FutureFuel Chemical Company, Batesville, AR

DOE/EA-1760
Environmental Assessment
August 2010

National Environmental Policy Act (NEPA) Compliance
Cover Sheet

Proposed Action:

The U.S. Department of Energy (DOE) proposes, through a cooperative agreement with FutureFuel Chemical Company (FutureFuel), to partially fund the design, installation and operations of a commercial-scale plant to produce intermediate anode material for high-performance lithium-ion (Li-ion) batteries. An existing FutureFuel manufacturing building would be retrofitted to accommodate the new plant in Batesville, Arkansas, and would support the anticipated growth in the electric drive vehicles (EDV) and hybrid-electric vehicle (HEV) industry. If approved, DOE would provide approximately 50 percent of the funding for the project.

Type of Statement: Draft Environmental Assessment (Draft EA or EA)

Lead Agency: U.S. Department of Energy (DOE); National Energy Technology Laboratory (NETL)

DOE Contact:

NEPA Information:	Project Information:
William Gwilliam	John Tabacchi
NEPA Document Manager	Project Manager
U.S. Department of Energy	U.S. Department of Energy
National Energy Technology Laboratory	National Energy Technology Laboratory
3610 Collins Ferry Road, P.O. Box 880	626 Cochrans Mill Roads, P.O. Box 10940
Morgantown, WV 26507-0880	Pittsburgh, PA 15236-0940
304-285-4401; 304-285-4403 (fax)	412-386-7298; 412-386-5835 (fax)
William.gwilliam@netl.doe.gov	John.Tabacchi@netl.doe.gov

Abstract:

DOE prepared this Environmental Assessment (EA) to assess the potential for impacts to the human and natural environment of its Proposed Action-providing financial assistance to FutureFuel under a cooperative agreement. DOE's objective is to support the development of the EDV industry in an effort to substantially reduce the United States' consumption of petroleum, in addition to stimulating the United States' economy. More specifically, DOE's objective is to accelerate the development and production of various EDV systems by building or increasing domestic manufacturing capacity for advanced automotive batteries, their components, recycling facilities, and EDV components. This work will enable market introduction of various electric vehicle technologies by lowering the cost of battery packs, batteries, and electric propulsion systems for EDVs through high-volume manufacturing.

Under the terms of the cooperative agreement, DOE would provide approximately 50 percent of the funding to FutureFuel to partially fund the retrofitting of an existing manufacturing building to a commercial-scale plant to produce intermediate anode material for high-performance Li-ion batteries (referred to as the "Proposed Project" within this EA). An existing FutureFuel manufacturing building (48,000 square feet, 5 stories) would be retrofitted to accommodate the proposed plant. The existing building that would be reconfigured currently includes over half of the major process equipment and pumps required to produce intermediate anode material. The goal would be to increase the product supply from the current 1,000,000 pounds per year at an off-site plant to 10,000,000 pounds per year, which would be sufficient for supplying over 2,000,000 HEVs. Additionally, the project would create approximately 33 permanent jobs.

The environmental analysis identified that the most notable changes, although minor, to result from FutureFuel's Proposed Project would occur in the following areas: air quality and greenhouse gas, surface water and groundwater, transportation and traffic, solid and hazardous wastes, and human health and safety. No significant environmental effects were identified in analyzing the potential consequences of these changes.

Electric Drive Vehicle Battery and
Component Manufacturing Initiative Project
FutureFuel Chemical Company, Batesville, AR

DOE/EA-1760
Environmental Assessment
August 2010

Public Participation:
DOE encourages public participation in the NEPA process. This EA was released for public review and comment. The public was invited to provide oral, written, or e-mail comments on this Draft EA to DOE by the close of the comment period on August 1, 2010. Copies of the Draft EA were also distributed to cognizant Federal and State agencies. Comments received by the close of the comment period were considered in preparing a Final EA for DOE Proposed Action. Public comments received on the EA are provided in Appendix B.

Electric Drive Vehicle Battery and
Component Manufacturing Initiative Project
FutureFuel Chemical Company, Batesville, AR

DOE/EA-1760
Environmental Assessment
August 2010

TABLE OF CONTENTS

Electric Drive Vehicle Battery and
Component Manufacturing Initiative Project
FutureFuel Chemical Company, Batesville, AR

DOE/EA-1760
Environmental Assessment
August 2010

LIST OF TABLES

LIST OF FIGURES

LIST OF APPENDICES

Appendix A – Agency Consultation
Appendix B – Public Comments on the Draft Environmental Assessment and Responses from the Department of Energy

Electric Drive Vehicle Battery and
Component Manufacturing Initiative Project
FutureFuel Chemical Company, Batesville, AR

DOE/EA-1760
Environmental Assessment
August 2010

ACRONYMS

Acronym	Definition
$\mu g/m^3$	microgram/per cubic meter
ADEQ	Arkansas Department of Environmental Quality
AST	aboveground storage tank
BMPs	best management practices
CAA	Clean Air Act
CX	categorically excluded
CFR	Code of Federal Regulations
CH_4	methane
CO	carbon monoxide
CO_2	carbon dioxide
CO_2e	carbon dioxide equivalent
°F	degrees Fahrenheit
DOE	U.S. Department of Energy
EA	Environmental Assessment
Eastman	Eastman SE, Incorporated
EDV	electric drive vehicle
EERE	Energy Efficiency and Renewable Energy
EIS	Environmental Impact Statement
EPA	U.S. Environmental Protection Agency
FONSI	Finding of No Significant Impact
FutureFuel	FutureFuel Chemical Company
GHG	greenhouse gases
HAP	hazardous air pollutants
HEV	hybrid-electric vehicle
HUC	Hydrologic Unit Code
Kgal	Kilo-gallon (1,000 gallons)
Li-ion	lithium-ion
MCL	maximum contaminant levels
mg	milligram
mg/l	milligrams per liter
mtpy	metric tons per year
NAAQS	National Ambient Air Quality Standards
NEPA	National Environmental Policy Act
NO_2	nitrogen dioxide
NO_x	nitrogen oxides
NPDES	National Pollution Discharge Elimination System
NWI	National Wetlands Inventory
O_3	ozone
Pb	lead

Electric Drive Vehicle Battery and
Component Manufacturing Initiative Project
FutureFuel Chemical Company, Batesville, AR

DOE/EA-1760
Environmental Assessment
August 2010

Acronym	Definition
PM	particulate matter
PM_{10}	particulate matter 10 microns or less
$PM_{2.5}$	particulate matter 2.5 microns or less
ppm	parts per million
PSD	prevention of significant deterioration
RADD	Remedial Action Decision Document
RFI	RCRA Facility Investigation
RCRA	Resource Conservation and Recovery Act
Recovery Act	American Recovery and Reinvestment Act of 2009, Public Law 111-5
RMP	Risk Management Plan
ROD	Record of Decision
SARA	Superfund Amendments and. Reauthorization Act
SWMU	solid waster management units
SIP	State Implementation Plan
SO_2	sulfur dioxide
SPCC	Spill Prevention, Control, and Countermeasures
std	Standard
tpy	tons per year
U.S.	United States
U.S.C.	United States Code
USFWS	U.S. Fish and Wildlife Service
VOCs	volatile organic compounds
VT	Vehicle Technologies
21	Enders stony fine sandy loam
39	Loring silt loam

Electric Drive Vehicle Battery and
Component Manufacturing Initiative Project
FutureFuel Chemical Company, Batesville, AR

DOE/EA-1760
Environmental Assessment
August 2010

1.0 PURPOSE AND NEED

1.1 Background

The U.S. Department of Energy (DOE or the Department) National Energy Technology Laboratory (NETL) manages the research and development portfolio of the Vehicle Technologies (VT) Program for the Office of Energy Efficiency and Renewable Energy (EERE). A key objective of the VT Program is accelerating the development and production of electric drive vehicle (EDV) systems to substantially reduce the United States' consumption of petroleum. Another of its goals is the development of production-ready batteries, power electronics, and electric machines that can be produced in volume economically to increase the use of EDVs.

Congress appropriated significant funding for the VT Program in the American Recovery and Reinvestment Act of 2009, Public Law 111-5 (Recovery Act) to stimulate the economy and reduce unemployment in addition to furthering the existing objectives of the VT Program. DOE solicited applications for this funding by issuing a competitive Funding Opportunity Announcement (DE-FOA-0000026), Recovery Act - Electric Drive Vehicle Battery and Component Manufacturing Initiative, on March 19, 2009. The announcement invited applications in seven areas of interest:

- Area of Interest 1 – Projects that would build or increase production capacity and validate production capability of advanced automotive battery manufacturing plants in the United States.
- Area of Interest 2 – Projects that would build or increase production capacity and validate production capability of anode and cathode active materials, components (e.g., separator, packaging material, electrolytes and salts), and processing equipment in domestic manufacturing plants.
- Area of Interest 3 – Projects that combine aspects of Areas of Interest 1 and 2.
- Area of Interest 4 – Projects that would build or increase production capacity and validate capability of domestic recycling or refurbishment plants for lithium-ion (Li-ion) batteries.
- Area of Interest 5 – Projects that would build or increase production capacity and validate production capability of advanced automotive electric drive components in domestic manufacturing plants.
- Area of Interest 6 – Projects that would build or increase production capacity and validate production capability of electric drive subcomponent suppliers in domestic manufacturing plants.
- Area of Interest 7 – Projects that combine aspects of Areas of Interest 5 and 6.

The application period closed on May 19, 2009, and DOE received 119 proposals across the seven areas of interest. DOE selected 30 projects based on the evaluation criteria set forth in the funding opportunity announcement; special consideration was given to projects that promoted the objectives of the Recovery Act – job preservation or creation and economic recovery – in an expeditious manner.

This project, proposed by the FutureFuel Chemical Company (FutureFuel), was one of the 30 projects that DOE selected for funding. The Department's Proposed Action is to provide $12.6 million in financial assistance in a cost-sharing arrangement with the project proponent FutureFuel. The total cost of the project is estimated at $25.2 million.

1.2 Purpose and Need for Department of Energy Action

The overall purpose and need for DOE action pursuant to the VT Program and the funding opportunity under the Recovery Act is to accelerate the development and production of various EDV systems by building or increasing domestic manufacturing capacity for advanced automotive batteries, recycling facilities, and EDV components, in addition to stimulating the United States' economy. This work will enable market introduction of various electric vehicle technologies by lowering the cost of battery packs, batteries, and electric propulsion systems for EDVs through high-volume manufacturing. DOE intends to further this purpose and satisfy this need by providing financial assistance under cost-sharing arrangements to this and the other 29 projects selected under this funding opportunity announcement.

Electric Drive Vehicle Battery and
Component Manufacturing Initiative Project
FutureFuel Chemical Company, Batesville, AR

DOE/EA-1760
Environmental Assessment
August 2010

This and the other selected projects are needed to reduce the United States' petroleum consumption by investing in alternative VTs. Successful commercialization of EDVs would support DOE's Energy Strategic Goal of "protect[ing] our national and economic security by promoting a diverse supply and delivery of reliable, affordable, and environmentally sound energy." This project will also meaningfully assist in the nation's economic recovery by creating manufacturing jobs in the United States in accordance with the objectives of the Recovery Act.

1.3 National Environmental Policy Act and Related Procedures

This Environmental Assessment (EA) is prepared in accordance with the National Environmental Policy Act (NEPA), as amended (42 U.S.C 4321), the President's Council on Environmental Quality regulations for implementing NEPA (40 Code of Federal Regulations [CFR] 1500-1508), and DOE's implementing procedures for compliance with NEPA (10 CFR 1021). This statute and the implementing regulations require that DOE, as a Federal agency:

- Assess the environmental impacts of any Proposed Action;
- Identify adverse environmental effects that cannot be avoided, should the Proposed Action be implemented;
- Evaluate alternatives to the Proposed Action, including a No Action Alternative; and
- Describe the cumulative impacts of the Proposed Action together with other past, present, and reasonably foreseeable future actions.

These provisions must be addressed before a decision is made to proceed with any proposed Federal action that has the potential to cause impacts to the human environment, including providing Federal funding to a project. This EA evaluates the potential individual and cumulative effects of the Proposed Project and the No Action Alternative on the physical, human, and natural environment. The EA is intended to meet DOE regulatory requirements under NEPA and provide DOE with the information needed to make an informed decision about providing financial assistance.

NEPA requires Federal agencies to take into account the potential consequences of their actions on both the natural and human environments as part of their planning and decision-making processes. To facilitate these considerations, a number of typical actions that have been determined to have little or no potential for adverse impacts are "categorically excluded" (CX) from the detailed NEPA assessment process. Thus, the first step in determining if an action would have an adverse effect on the environment is to assess whether it fits into a defined category for which a CX is applicable. If a CX is applied, the agency prepares a Record of Categorical Exclusion to document the decision and proceeds with the action.

For actions that are not subject to a CX, the agency prepares an EA to determine the potential for significant impacts. If through the evaluation and analysis conducted for the EA process, it is determined that no significant impacts would occur as a result of the action, then the determination would result in a Finding of No Significant Impact (FONSI). The Federal agency would then publish an EA and the FONSI. The NEPA process is complete when the FONSI is executed.

If significant adverse impacts to the natural or human environment are indicated or other intervening circumstances either exist at the onset of a project or are determined through the EA process, an Environmental Impact Statement (EIS) may be prepared. An EIS is a more intensive study of the effects of the Proposed Action.

Electric Drive Vehicle Battery and
Component Manufacturing Initiative Project
FutureFuel Chemical Company, Batesville, AR

DOE/EA-1760
Environmental Assessment
August 2010

1.4   Agency Coordination

DOE conducted consultations with the Arkansas Department of Arkansas Heritage, the U.S. Fish and Wildlife Service (USFWS), and the Natural Heritage Program, pursuant to of Section 106 of the National Historic Preservation Act and Section 7 of the Endangered Species Act, respectively. The consultation letters are included in Appendix A of this EA.

Electric Drive Vehicle Battery and
Component Manufacturing Initiative Project
FutureFuel Chemical Company, Batesville, AR

DOE/EA-1760
Environmental Assessment
August 2010

This page intentionally left blank.

Electric Drive Vehicle Battery and
Component Manufacturing Initiative Project
FutureFuel Chemical Company, Batesville, AR

DOE/EA-1760
Environmental Assessment
August 2010

2.0 PROPOSED ACTION AND ALTERNATIVES

2.1 Department of Energy's Proposed Action

DOE proposes, through a cooperative agreement with FutureFuel, to partially fund the design, installation, and operations of a commercial-scale plant to produce intermediate anode material for high-performance Li-ion batteries. An existing FutureFuel manufacturing building would be retrofitted to accommodate the new plant in Batesville, Arkansas and would support the anticipated growth in the hybrid-electric vehicle (HEV) industry. If approved, DOE would provide approximately 50 percent of the funding for the project.

2.2 FutureFuel's Proposed Project

FutureFuel proposes to design, install, and operate a commercial-scale plant to produce intermediate anode material (a coated and dried petroleum coke) for high-performance Li-ion batteries. An existing FutureFuel manufacturing building (48,000 square feet, 5 stories) would be retrofitted to accommodate the proposed plant. The existing building that would be reconfigured currently includes over half of the major process equipment and pumps required to produce intermediate anode material. The goal would be to increase the product supply from the current 1,000,000 pounds per year at an off-site semi-works plant to 10,000,000 pounds per year. Figure 2.2-1 depicts the proposed FutureFuel anode material production process. Upon completion in 2011, the plant would have the capacity to process 10,000,000 pounds per year of intermediate anode material sufficient for supplying over 2,000,000 HEVs.

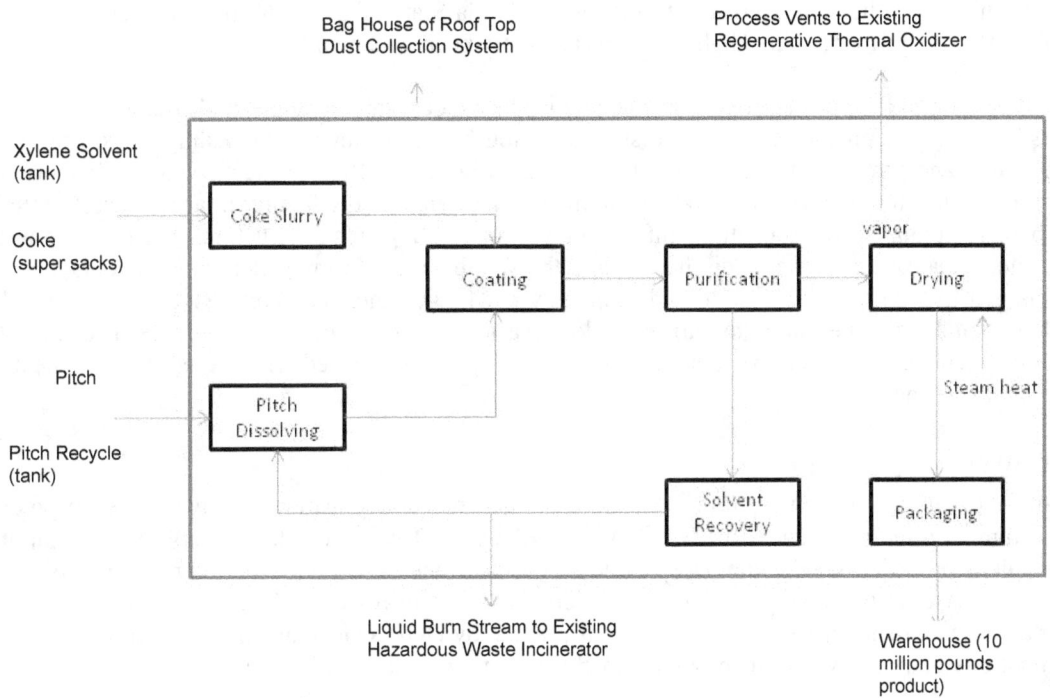

Figure 2.2-1 Proposed FutureFuel Production Process

Electric Drive Vehicle Battery and
Component Manufacturing Initiative Project
FutureFuel Chemical Company, Batesville, AR

DOE/EA-1760
Environmental Assessment
August 2010

The Proposed Project would include using an existing building, formerly utilitized to produce a bleach activator. Most of the modifications would be limited to changes to reactors, pumps, piping, centrifuges, dryers, process vent systems, and instrumentation for process equipment located inside the existing building. Outside of the plant, a concrete loading dock would be added on the southeastern corner; a nitrogen air separator unit package plant would be installed in the utilities area adjacent to other infrastructure to the east, to supply nitrogen to the anode material dryer; and to the west of the existing tank farm, two 35,000-gallon above ground tanks (ASTs) would also be installed on a concrete pad with vertical concrete containment walls. The two ASTs would be used to store xylene and petroleum pitch that would be used in the manufacturing process. The nitrogen air separator unit package plant, including absorbers, would be 14 feet wide by 14 feet long by 20 feet tall and would be installed on a new concrete pad approximately 54 feet by 23 feet at a previously graded utility area. The separator unit package plant, similar to an Air Products Model PSA-195A3, would involve two compressor and air and nitrogen surge tanks.

2.3 General Description and Location

The Proposed Project would be located at the FutureFuel Chemical Facility approximately 8 miles east, southeast of Batesville, in Independence County, Arkansas (Figure 2.3-1). The existing facility is located on Gap Road (State Highway 394), and currently produces biodiesel and specialty chemical products (e.g., bleach activator, pesticides, polymer modifiers, coating additives). The facility consists of approximately 400 acres of developed land which is located on a 2,200-acre campus. The property is bounded by the White River to the south, Russell Ferry Road to the west, Gap Road to the north, and Barber Road to the east. The area surrounding the existing FutureFuel facility is characterized by wooded areas with dispersed residential properties, with the exception of the White River which is to the south. Access to the facility is via State Highway 69 from Batesville (west) or Newport (southeast), to Gap Road. State Highway 69 has recently been widened.

The 400 acres of developed land of the campus is characterized by industrial operations and equipment, including various process building, equipment (e.g., ASTs, distillers, piping, etc.), loading and unloading areas, warehouses and storage buildings, and administrative and security buildings (Figure 2.3-2). The site also has a rail spur which is used for various chemical deliveries and product shipments that transects the facility in an east/west direction. The facility obtains cooling water from the White River via an existing intake structure, and treats industrial wastewater on-site. Treated wastewater is discharged into the White River. Storm water and non-contact cooling water are discharged to a large holding pond and ultimately discharged into the White River. There are three coal-fired boilers (that are also permitted to burn hazardous waste) used to produce steam and heat for industrial use. There are two coal ash ponds on the western side of the property associated with these boilers. The site is fenced and has controlled access.

2.4 Alternatives

DOE's alternatives to this project consist of the 45 technically acceptable applications received in response to the Funding Opportunity Announcement, Recovery Act - Electric Drive Vehicle Battery and Component Manufacturing Initiative. Prior to selection, DOE made preliminary determinations regarding the level of review required by NEPA based on potentially significant impacts identified in reviews of acceptable applications. A variance to certain requirements in 10 CFR 1021.216 was granted by DOE's General Counsel. These preliminary NEPA determinations and reviews were provided to the selecting official, who considered them during the selection process.

Because DOE's Proposed Action is limited to providing financial assistance in cost-sharing arrangements to projects submitted by applicants in response to a competitive funding opportunity, DOE's decision is limited to either accepting or rejecting the project as proposed by the proponent, including its proposed technology and selected sites. DOE's consideration of reasonable alternatives is therefore limited to the technically acceptable applications and a No Action Alternative for each selected project.

Electric Drive Vehicle Battery and
Component Manufacturing Initiative Project
FutureFuel Chemical Company, Batesville, AR

DOE/EA-1760
Environmental Assessment
August 2010

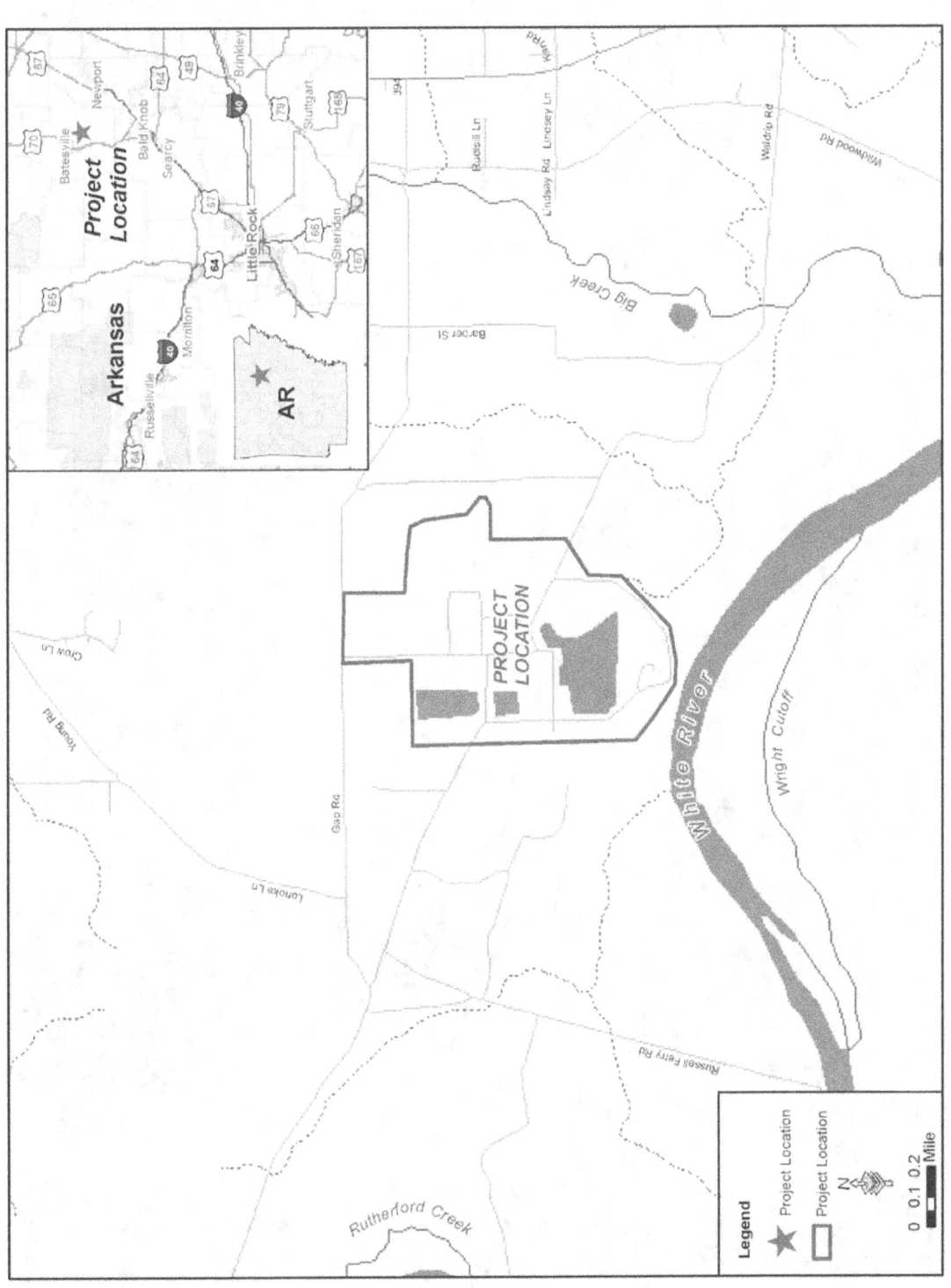

Figure 2.3-1. Regional Location Map

DOE/EA-1760
Environmental Assessment
August 2010

Electric Drive Vehicle Battery and
Component Manufacturing Initiative Project
FutureFuel Chemical Company, Batesville, AR

Figure 2.3-2. Site Location Map

Electric Drive Vehicle Battery and
Component Manufacturing Initiative Project
FutureFuel Chemical Company, Batesville, AR

DOE/EA-1760
Environmental Assessment
August 2010

2.5   No Action Alternative

Under the No Action Alternative, DOE would not provide funds to this Proposed Project. As a result, this project would be delayed while the applicant seeks other funding sources. Alternatively, the applicant would abandon this project if other funding sources are not obtained. Furthermore, acceleration of the development and production of various EDV systems would not occur or would be delayed. DOE's ability to achieve its objectives under the VT Program and the Recovery Act would be reduced.

Although this and other selected projects might proceed if DOE decided not to provide financial assistance, DOE assumes for purposes of this environmental analysis that the project would not proceed without DOE assistance. If projects did proceed without DOE's financial assistance, the potential impacts would be essentially identical to those under DOE's action alternative (i.e., providing financial assistance that allows the project to proceed). In order to allow a comparison between the potential impacts of a project as implemented and the impacts of not proceeding with a project, DOE assumes that if it were to decide to withhold assistance from a project, the project would not proceed.

2.6   Alternatives Considered by FutureFuel

The FutureFuel facility has an existing building and the equipment already in place to accommodate the Proposed Project. Therefore, no other alternatives were considered other than the No Action Alternative.

2.7   Summary of Environmental Consequences

Table 2.7-1 provides a summary of the environmental, cultural, and socioeconomic impacts of the No Action and the Proposed Project.

Table 2.7-1. Summary of Environmental, Cultural, and Socioeconomic Impacts

Impact Area	No Action Alternative		Proposed Project	
	Construction	Operations	Construction	Operations
Land Use	Negligible	Negligible	Negligible	Negligible
Meteorology	Negligible	Negligible	Negligible	Negligible
Socioeconomics (Population and Housing)	Negligible	Negligible	Negligible	Negligible
Socioeconomics (Taxes, Revenue, Economy, Employment)	Negligible	Negligible	Minor Beneficial	Minor Beneficial
Environmental Justice	Negligible	Negligible	Negligible	Negligible
Visual Resources	Negligible	Negligible	Negligible	Negligible
Cultural Resources	Negligible	Negligible	Negligible	Negligible
Geology and Soils	Negligible	Negligible	Negligible	Negligible
Wetlands and Floodplains	Negligible	Negligible	Negligible	Negligible
Vegetation and Wildlife	Negligible	Negligible	Negligible	Negligible
Noise	Negligible	Negligible	Negligible	Negligible
Utilities and Energy Use	Negligible	Negligible	Negligible	Negligible
Air Quality	Negligible	Negligible	Minor	Minor
Greenhouse Gases	Negligible	Moderate	Minor	Beneficial
Surface Water	Negligible	Negligible	Minor	Negligible
Groundwater	Negligible	Negligible	Minor	Minor
Transportation and Traffic	Negligible	Negligible	Minor	Minor
Solid and Hazardous Waste	Negligible	Negligible	Negligible	Minor
Human Health and Safety	Negligible	Negligible	Negligible	Minor

Electric Drive Vehicle Battery and
Component Manufacturing Initiative Project
FutureFuel Chemical Company, Batesville, AR

DOE/EA-1760
Environmental Assessment
August 2010

This page intentionally left blank.

Electric Drive Vehicle Battery and
Component Manufacturing Initiative Project
FutureFuel Chemical Company, Batesville, AR

DOE/EA-1760
Environmental Assessment
August 2010

3.0 AFFECTED ENVIRONMENT AND ENVIRONMENTAL CONSEQUENCES

Chapter 3 provides a description of the affected environment (existing conditions) at the project site and a discussion of the environmental consequences of the No Action Alternative and the Proposed Project. Additionally, cumulative impacts and mitigation measures are discussed where appropriate. The methodology used to identify existing conditions and to evaluate potential impacts on the physical and human environment involved the following: review of the Environmental Questionnaire and the Project Narrative prepared by FutureFuel; review of other documentation provided by FutureFuel (FutureFuel, 2010a); searches of various environmental databases; agency consultations; and a site visit conducted on April 12, 2010.

3.1 Resource Areas Dismissed from Further Consideration

DOE has determined that various resources would either not be affected or would sustain negligible impacts from FutureFuel's Proposed Project and do not require further evaluation. They include land use, meteorology, socioeconomics, environmental justice, visual resources, cultural resources, geology and soils, wetlands and floodplains, vegetation and wildlife, noise, utilities and energy use; therefore, these resource areas are briefly discussed in this section of the EA and will not be evaluated further.

Land Use: The Proposed Project would not result in impacts to land use and zoning. According to information collected during the site visit, the land use designation for the proposed site is Industrial. Therefore, no change in land use designation would be required for the Proposed Project.

Meteorology: Generally, Arkansas has hot, humid summers and cold, slightly drier winters. In Batesville, the daily high temperatures average around 92 degrees Fahrenheit (°F) with lows around 69°F in the month of July. In January highs average around 45°F and lows around 25°F. Annual precipitation throughout the State averages between about 40 and 60 inches. Snowfall is common in the north half of the Arkansas, which usually gets several snowfalls each winter. This is not only due to its closer proximity to the plains states, but also to the higher elevations found throughout the Ozark and Ouachita mountains. Due to the geographical location, operations would not be affected by severe weather events, such as hurricanes or tornadoes, because they are not likely to occur and therefore, would have no impact on the plant operations.

Socioeconomics: The Proposed Project would result in the hiring of approximately 33 permanent jobs. It is assumed that the majority of the workforce would be drawn from local candidates; therefore, no increase in population or need for housing is anticipated. Negligible impacts to housing and population are anticipated.

Under the Proposed Project, taxes would continue to be paid on the property and no adverse impacts would occur. Workers employed for the construction period (approximately 100 construction jobs) are assumed to be currently employed, and residing and paying taxes in the Independence County, Arkansas area. Increased sales transactions for the purchase of materials and supplies would generate some additional revenues for local and State governments, which would have a negligible, but beneficial impact on taxes and revenue.

Secondary jobs related to the increased economic activity stimulated by the Proposed Project may be created. Additional retail services and business employment may result through a multiplier effect, yielding additional sales and income tax revenues for local and State governments, thus having a minor, but beneficial impact.

Construction of the project would not result in direct impacts to community facilities, services, school systems, or emergency services of Batesville, Arkansas because significant numbers of employees are not anticipated to relocate as a result of the Proposed Project. Therefore, negligible impacts to community facilities and services are anticipated.

Environmental Justice: FutureFuel's Proposed Project was evaluated in accordance with EO 12898 Federal Actions Address Environmental Justice in Minority Populations and Low-Income Populations. While there are

Electric Drive Vehicle Battery and
Component Manufacturing Initiative Project
FutureFuel Chemical Company, Batesville, AR

DOE/EA-1760
Environmental Assessment
August 2010

minority and low-income populations in the study area, FutureFuel's Proposed Project would not have a disproportionately adverse impact on these groups.

Visual Resources: The Proposed Project site is located on a 2,200-acre property, of which 400 acres has been converted for industrial use as a manufacturing plant. The proposed site is within the 400-acre manufacturing plant, and is bounded on all sides by existing industrial infrastructure. Impacts to identified views and vistas were determined based on an analysis of the existing quality of the landscape views, the sensitivity of the view, and the anticipated relationship of the scale and massing of the proposed buildings to the existing visual environment. New construction is not expected to be noticeable outside the plant boundaries, and would be consistent with existing buildings at the manufacturing plant.

Cultural Resources: The Proposed Project involves the retrofit of an existing building, construction of a loading dock, installation of a nitrogen air separator unit package plant, and addition of two ASTs. The Area of Potential Effect (APE) for archaeological resources is defined as the construction impact area. It is unlikely that archaeological resources are present within the APE, as the land has been previously disturbed. The APE for architectural resources is defined as being approximately 0.5 miles of the perimeter of the existing facility boundaries. There are no known structures within the APE over 50 years of age. Therefore, no impacts to historic or cultural properties are anticipated, thus, DOE has made a finding of No Historic Properties Effected for this undertaking. In a letter dated May 4, 2010 (Appendix A), from the Arkansas Historic Preservation Program, four archaeological sites on the FutureFuel property were identified. However, the sites were determined to be ineligible for inclusion into the National Register of Historic Places, due to being previously damaged and destroyed by construction activities. Therefore, the Arkansas State Historic Preservation Officer has concurred with DOE's finding of No Historic Properties Effected.

Geology and Soils: The main geological landforms present within the project site include hill slope and terrace. Hill slopes are characterized by relatively steeply sloping terrain (8 to 20 percent slopes). Terraces are step like surfaces, bordering a valley floor or shoreline that represents the former position of a floodplain (i.e., the White River). The Independence County Soil Survey (NRCS, 2008) indicates two soil types within proximity to the project site, which include Enders stony fine sandy loam (21), 8 to 20 percent slopes and Loring silt loam (39), 3 to 8 percent slopes. Soils within the project site are not prone to flooding. No mapped hydric soils occur within the project site.

In a letter dated May 12, 2010 (see Appendix A), the USFWS expressed concerns regarding the potential for caves, sinkholes, springs, losing streams, and underground passages occurring on or near the project site due to the regional karst topography. Impacts to these resources could have the potential to adversely impact Federally-protected endangered species (see *Vegetation and Wildlife* for a listing of Federally-endangered species in Independence County). None of these resources are known to occur at the project site.

The April 12, 2010, site visit of the study area revealed the project site is a combination of existing developed land and previously graded land, primarily covered by impervious surface. Both development and grading has caused considerable disturbance to the soils (i.e., sloping no longer exists within the project site and properties limiting commercial construction building have likely been altered). As the Proposed Project involves the retrofit of an existing facility, negligible impacts to soils would be anticipated from both construction and operations. Furthermore, negligible impacts would be anticipated to caves, sinkholes, springs, losing streams, and underground passages occurring on or near the project site as the Proposed Project retrofits would occur within existing facilities and developed sites.

Wetlands and Floodplains: National Wetlands Inventory (NWI) mapping does not indicate the presence of wetlands within the project site (USFWS, 2010). In addition, the Independence County Soil Survey did not indicate the presence of hydric soils within the project site, a potential indicator that wetlands could be present. The April 12, 2010, site visit verified no apparent wetlands were located within the project site. One manmade

Electric Drive Vehicle Battery and
Component Manufacturing Initiative Project
FutureFuel Chemical Company, Batesville, AR

DOE/EA-1760
Environmental Assessment
August 2010

pond is located directly south of the project site within the FutureFuel property. This pond is used to temper non-contact cooling water prior to discharge into the White River. NWI mapping verifies this pond is excavated and, therefore, would not be considered jurisdictional as it is manmade and serves industrial use.

The Federal Emergency Management Agency, Flood Insurance Rate Map Number 05063C0375D does not indicate the presence of floodplain within the project site (FEMA, 2010). Areas of floodplain, however, do occur to the south of the project site and are associated with the White River; these areas of floodplain would not be affected by the Proposed Project.

Vegetation and Wildlife: The April 12, 2010, site visit of the project site revealed the majority of the site is already developed or has been rough graded and contains maintained grassy vegetation. The vegetation within the project site, therefore, has been completely removed or altered from historical natural communities which consisted of eastern broadleaf forest province vegetation (oak-hickory forest associations). No wildlife species were observed within the project site during the April 12, 2010, site visit. Due to the man-altered characteristics of historical vegetation communities, no wildlife habitat value exists within the project site; the remaining maintained grassy areas provides little to no habitat.

Informal coordination letters have been sent to both the USFWS and the Arkansas Natural Heritage Commission to verify the project would have no impact on any Federally- or State-listed threatened, endangered, or candidate species, or critical habitat within the vicinity of FutureFuel's Proposed Project (see Appendix A). In a letter dated April 16, 2010, the Arkansas Natural Heritage Commission stated at present, no records of rare, threatened, or endangered species exist within the project site. The USFWS stated in a letter dated May 12, 2010, that the following endangered species are known to occur in Independence County: Gray bat *(Myotis grisescenss),* Indiana bat *(Myotis sodalisi),* Pink mucket *(Lampsilis abrupta),* and Running buffalo clover *(Trifolium stoloniferumi).* The USFWS determined the Proposed Project is not likely to adversely affect these listed species provided adverse impacts to caves, sinkholes, springs, losing streams, and underground passages are avoided (see Geology and Soils discussion) and the Proposed Project minimizes adverse impacts to surface and groundwater quality (see Section 3.2.2.2.2). Overall, the Proposed Project avoids impacts to these resources; therefore, impacts to these species would be negligible.

Noise: The proposed site is an industrial complex that consists of approximately 400 acres of developed land located on a campus of approximately 2,200 acres. The property is bounded by the White River to the south, Russell Ferry Road to the west, Gap Road (State Highway 394) to the north, and Waldrip Road to the east. The area surrounding the FutureFuel site is characterized by wooded areas with dispersed residential properties. The developed land of the industrial complex is characterized by industrial operations and equipment, including various process buildings, equipment (e.g., ASTs, distillers, piping, etc.), loading and unloading areas, warehouses and storage buildings, and administrative and security buildings. The nearest sensitive receptors to noise are the few scattered homes located in the wooded areas around the property. The nearest residences are located over 0.6 miles to the east and northeast. The nearest church is located approximately 1.5 miles to the east, and there are no schools located closer than 3 miles to the site (EPA, 2010a).

There are existing noise sources in the vicinity that contribute to the baseline noise level, including vehicle traffic from the nearby highways, as well as train noise from the railroad spur that transects the FutureFuel property and meets up with the main railroad line along State Highway 69 located approximately 1.6 miles to the east of the site. In addition, there is consistent truck and vehicle traffic accessing the site daily (approximately 110 to 165 trucks per week) as well as noise from existing building mechanical equipment, loading docks, outdoor components of ventilation systems, pumps, etc. (FutureFuel, 2010a).

Short-term but measurable adverse impacts to noise are expected during the construction phase of the project. Most of the site modifications would be limited to changes to reactors, piping, and other process equipment located inside an existing building, as well as the construction of a loading dock and concrete pad, and installation

Electric Drive Vehicle Battery and
Component Manufacturing Initiative Project
FutureFuel Chemical Company, Batesville, AR

DOE/EA-1760
Environmental Assessment
August 2010

of the nitrogen air separator unit package plant, and two ASTs. During the construction phase, noise levels would be localized, intermittent, and temporary. Increases in noise levels during construction would mainly result from the use of heavy construction equipment and delivery trucks, as well as increased traffic due to construction workers accessing the site. The typical noise levels at any construction site would be expected to be within the range of 75 to 90 decibels. Construction noise levels onsite would primarily be limited to the immediate vicinity of the project site, and the majority of the construction would occur indoors. Construction noise should be negligible from the perspective of the nearest sensitive receptors (a few homes) as they are located over a half mile away, with a buffer of wooded areas between them and the project site. The construction is expected to last for approximately 13 months.

The main sources of noise during operations would be from additional truck and employee-vehicle traffic and from the new loading dock and nitrogen air separator unit package plant. The Proposed Project expects to increase traffic to and from the site by approximately 15 trucks per week, and additional personal vehicle traffic from approximately 33 new employees (FutureFuel, 2010a). The new process equipment for the project would be predominantly located indoors, with the exception of the nitrogen air separator unit package plant.

Because the Proposed Project is an addition to an existing industrial facility that currently has truck and personal-vehicle traffic, loading docks, compressors, outdoor equipment, and numerous building mechanical systems, any increase in ambient noise levels resulting from operations would be negligible from the perspective of any sensitive receptors in the surrounding area. Furthermore, the sensitive receptors are currently exposed to noise from the railroad and highway traffic.

Utilities and Energy Use: The FutureFuel property is located within the service area of Rock-Moore Water Association from which it receives its potable water supply. The Rock-Moore Water Association takes its water supply from wells, and currently produces an average of 450,000 gallons per day of potable water (Rock-Moore Water Association, 2010). Process water for the FutureFuel facility is drawn from the White River. All wastewater from the FutureFuel facility is routed to an onsite wastewater treatment facility through a system of drains, sumps, pipes, and other collection devices; it is treated then discharged to the White River. During construction for the Proposed Project, utilities would be supplied by existing services at the FutureFuel facility, which would not be adversely impacted by the small increases in temporary demand.

FutureFuel anticipates adding an additional 33 employees under the Proposed Action (FutureFuel, 2010). During operations, these employees would use approximately 430 gallons per day of potable water per day (at an average of 13 gallons per day per employee at an industrial facility) (Lin and Liptak, 1997). This increased demand would equate to approximately 0.09 percent of the Rock-Moore Water Association capacity for water supply, and therefore, the impacts on water utilities would be negligible.

All process water would be drawn from the White River. Wastewater from the FutureFuel facility would be treated by the onsite wastewater treatment facility for ultimate discharge to the White River. The expansion of the FutureFuel Facility would have no impact on local wastewater municipalities. See Section 3.2.2, Surface Water, for discussion of impacts on the White River.

The City of Batesville is located within the service area of Entergy Power Company, which has over 15,500 miles of high-voltage transmission lines and 1,550 transmission substations, and spans portions of four states. Entergy owns and operates power plants with a total electric generating capacity of approximately 30,000 megawatts (Entergy Power, 2010). The FutureFuel facility would have an estimated power consumption of approximately 732 megawatt hours per month. This would represent less than 0.01 percent of Entergy Power Companies generating capacity. Although Entergy Power Company should be consulted, the impacts on electrical utilities should be negligible (FutureFuel, 2010a; Entergy Power, 2010).

Electric Drive Vehicle Battery and
Component Manufacturing Initiative Project
FutureFuel Chemical Company, Batesville, AR

DOE/EA-1760
Environmental Assessment
August 2010

3.2   Resource Areas Considered Further

Environmental resource areas carried through for further consideration of the potential impact of FutureFuel's Proposed Project include air quality and greenhouse gas, surface water and groundwater, transportation and traffic, solid and hazardous waste, and human health and safety.

3.2.1   Air Quality and Greenhouse Gas

Air Quality Management

The purpose of the air quality analysis is to determine whether emissions from a proposed new or modified source of air pollution, in conjunction with emissions from existing sources, would cause or contribute to the deterioration of the air quality in the area. The Clean Air Act (CAA) requires the U.S. Environmental Protection Agency (EPA) to set National Ambient Air Quality Standards (NAAQS) for pollutants considered harmful to public health and the environment. NAAQS include two types of air quality standards (40 CFR 50.1(e)). Primary standards protect public health, including the health of sensitive populations such as asthmatics, children, and the elderly. Secondary standards protect public welfare, including protection against decreased visibility, damage to animals, crops, vegetation, and buildings. EPA has established NAAQS for six principal pollutants, which are called "criteria pollutants": ozone (O_3), carbon monoxide (CO), nitrogen dioxide (NO_2), particulate matter (PM), particulate matter 10 microns or less (PM_{10}), particulate matter 2.5 microns or less ($PM_{2.5}$), sulfur dioxide (SO_2) and lead (Pb). Table 3.2.1-1 lists the NAAQS.

Table 3.2.1-1. National Ambient Air Quality Standards

Pollutant	Standard	Averaging Time	Standard Type
CO	35 ppm (40 mg/m^3)	1-hour	Primary
	9 ppm (10 mg/m^3)	8-hour	
Pb	0.15 µg/m^3	Rolling 3-Month Average[1]	Primary and Secondary
	1.5 µg/m3	Quarterly Average	
NO$_2$	53 ppb	Annual (Arithmetic Mean)	Primary and Secondary
	100 ppb	1-hour [2]	Primary
PM$_{2.5}$	35 µg/m^3	24-hour	Primary and Secondary
	15.0 µg/m^3	Annual (Arithmetic Mean)	
PM$_{10}$	150 µg/m^3	24-hour	Primary and Secondary
SO$_2$	0.5 ppm (1300 µg/m^3)	3-hour	Secondary
	0.14 ppm	24-hour	Primary
	0.03 ppm	Annual (Arithmetic Mean)	
O$_3$	0.12 ppm	1-hour[3]	Primary and Secondary
	0.075 ppm (2008 std)	8-hour	
	0.08 ppm (1997 std)	8-hour[4]	

(1) Final rule signed October 15, 2008.
(2) Effective January 22, 2010.
(3) As of June 15, 2005. 1-hour O_3 was revoked in all areas except 14 8-hour O_3 nonattainment Early Action Compact Areas. Independence County, Arkansas is not an Early Action Compact Areas.
(4) The 1997 standard and its implementation rules would remain in place as EPA undertakes rulemaking to address the transition to the 2008 standard.
µg/m^3 – microgram/per cubic meter; mg/m^3 – milligram/per cubic meter; ppm – parts per million; std – standard.
Source: EPA, 2010b

To determine compliance with the NAAQS, emissions of criteria pollutants from a new or modified source(s) are modeled to determine their air dispersion concentrations. In addition to the six criteria pollutants outlined in the CAA, several other substances raise concerns with regard to air quality and are regulated through the CAA

Electric Drive Vehicle Battery and
Component Manufacturing Initiative Project
FutureFuel Chemical Company, Batesville, AR

DOE/EA-1760
Environmental Assessment
August 2010

Amendments of 1990. These substances include hazardous air pollutants (HAPs) and toxic air pollutants (such as metals, nitrogen oxides (NO_X), and volatile organic compounds (VOCs). NO_X and VOCs are precursors for O_3.

Areas that meet the air quality standard for the criteria pollutants are designated as being in attainment. Areas that do not meet the air quality standard for one or more of the criteria pollutants are designated as being in nonattainment for that standard. The CAA requires nonattainment states to submit to the EPA a State Implementation Plan (SIP) for attainment of the NAAQS (40 CFR 51.166, 40 CFR 93). Maintenance areas are those that at one point had not met the NAAQS but are currently maintaining the standards through the requirements in the SIP.

The 1990 Amendments to the CAA require Federal actions to show conformance with the SIP. Federal actions are those projects that are funded by Federal agencies and include the review and approval of a Proposed Project through the NEPA process. Conformance with the SIP means conformity to the approved SIP's purpose of eliminating or reducing the severity and number of violations of the NAAQS and achieving expeditious attainment of such standards (40 CFR, 51 and 93). The need to demonstrate conformity is applicable only to nonattainment and maintenance areas.

Class I Areas and Sensitive Receptors

For areas that are already in compliance with the NAAQS, the Prevention of Significant Deterioration (PSD) requirements provide maximum allowable increases in concentrations of pollutants, which are expressed as increments (40 CFR 52.21). Allowable PSD increments currently exist for three pollutants: SO_2, NO_2, and PM_{10} (Table 3.2.1-2).

Table 3.2.1-2. Allowable Prevention of Significant Deterioration Increments ($\mu g/m^3$)

Pollutant-- Averaging Period	Class I Area	Class II Area
SO_2--3-Hour	25	512
--24-Hour	5	91
--Annual	2	20
NO_2--Annual	2.5	25
PM_{10}--24-Hour	8	30
--Annual	4	17

Source: 40 CFR 52.21(c)

One set of allowable increments exists for Class II areas, which covers most of the United States and another set of more stringent allowable increments exists for Class I areas. Because of their pristine environment, Class I areas require more rigorous safeguards to prevent deterioration of their air quality. For the purposes of PSD review, the Federal government has identified mandatory Class I areas, which as defined in the CAA, are the following that were in existence as of August 7, 1977: national parks over 6,000 acres, national wilderness areas and national memorial parks over 5,000 acres, and international parks (NPS, 2009a). In general, proposed projects that are within 62 miles of Class I areas must evaluate impacts of the project on air quality related values (AQRVs) such as visibility, flora/fauna, water quality, soils, odor, and any other resources specified by the Federal Land Manager (NPS, 2009b).

Areas that are not in attainment with NAAQS are subject to the Nonattainment New Source Review. Overall, for the purposes of air quality analysis, any area to which the general public has access is considered a sensitive receptor site, and includes residences, day care centers, educational and health facilities, places of worship, parks, and playgrounds.

Electric Drive Vehicle Battery and
Component Manufacturing Initiative Project
FutureFuel Chemical Company, Batesville, AR

DOE/EA-1760
Environmental Assessment
August 2010

Greenhouse Gases

Greenhouse Gases (GHGs) are pollutants of concern for air quality and climate change. GHGs include water vapor, CO_2, methane (CH_4), NO_X, O_3, and several chlorofluorocarbons. Water vapor is a naturally occurring GHG and accounts for the largest percentage of the greenhouse effect. Next to water vapor, CO_2 is the second-most abundant GHG and is typically produced from human-related activities. The largest source of CO_2 emissions globally is the combustion of fossil fuels such as coal, oil, and gas in power plants, automobiles, industrial facilities and other sources. Additionally, a number of specialized industrial production processes and product uses such as mineral production, metal production and the use of petroleum-based products can also lead to CO_2 emissions. The manufacturing of electrode materials for ultra capacitors can produce CO_2 emissions.

Although regulatory agencies are taking actions to address GHG effects, there are currently no State or Federal standards or regulations limiting CO_2 emissions and concentrations in the ambient air. In response to the *FY2008 Consolidated Appropriations Act* (House Resolution 2764; Public Law 110–161), EPA issued the *Final Mandatory Reporting of Greenhouse Gases Rule* (GHG Reporting Rule), which became effective on January 1, 2010. The GHG Reporting Rule requires annual reporting of GHG emissions to EPA from large sources and suppliers in the United States, including suppliers of fossil fuels or industrial GHGs; manufacturers of vehicles and engines; and facilities that emit greater than 25,000 metric tons per year (mtpy) (27,558 tons per year [tpy]) each of CO_2 and other GHGs. The intent of the rule is to collect accurate and timely emissions data to inform future policy decisions and programs to reduce emissions, as well as fight against the effects of climate change.

Additionally, on September 30, 2009, EPA proposed, under the CAA, new thresholds for GHG that would require that facilities subjected to the New Source Review and Title V operating permit programs to obtain permits and would cover nearly 70 percent of the nation's largest stationary source GHG emitters—including power plants, refineries, and cement production facilities, while shielding small businesses and farms from permitting requirements. The proposed thresholds are currently being reviewed by Congress.

3.2.1.1 Affected Environment

Air Quality

The Arkansas Department of Environmental Quality (ADEQ), Air Division is responsible for monitoring air quality for each of the criteria pollutants and assessing compliance. The Arkansas Pollution Control & Ecology Commission Regulations are promulgated in Regulations 7, 9, 18, 19, 26, and 31. Independence County is in attainment for all criteria air pollutants, including the new 8-hour ozone standard (EPA, 2010c; EPA, 2010d); therefore, DOE does not need to demonstrate conformity with the Arkansas SIP for this project.

There are two Federal mandatory Class I areas in Arkansas (i.e., Caney Creek Wilderness Area and Upper Buffalo Wilderness Area), for which the ADEQ requires a PSD review to determine potential impact. Neither of these Class I areas are within 62 miles from the Proposed Project. The nearest sensitive receptors are the few scattered homes located in the wooded areas around the property. The nearest residences are located over 0.6 miles to the east and northeast. The nearest church is located approximately 1.5 miles to the east, and there are no schools located closer than 3 miles to the site (EPA, 2010e).

Current Air Emissions

FutureFuel currently has a Title V Major Source Permit issued by the ADEQ (FutureFuel, 2010a; ADEQ, 2004a). The permit, Permit No. 1085-AOP-R8, applies to all equipment and activities, including fugitive emissions, associated with the industrial chemical manufacturing facility located at the site.. A Title V Major Source Permit is granted to a facility that has the potential to emit more than 100 tpy of any of the six criteria pollutants, or more than 10 tpy of any single HAP or more than 25 tpy of any combination of HAPs. Although the permit expired in January 2009, FutureFuel submitted a permit renewal application which was accepted in June 2008 and the facility is under a permit shield until the revised permit becomes effective.

Table 3.2.1-3 provides the maximum emissions rate allowed at the FutureFuel facility.

Electric Drive Vehicle Battery and
Component Manufacturing Initiative Project
FutureFuel Chemical Company, Batesville, AR

DOE/EA-1760
Environmental Assessment
August 2010

Table 3.2.1-3. Current Permitted Emissions for FutureFuel Operations

Pollutant	Total Allowable Emissions (tpy)
PM_{10}	342.1
SO_2	6,314.6
VOC	639.4
CO	1,864.4
NO_X	794.7
Inorganics HAPs	940.0
Organic HAPs	639.6

Source: FutureFuel, 2010a; ADEQ, 2004a

For 2009, the FutureFuel facility produced 378,954 mtpy (417,725 tpy) of CO_2: energy consumption (i.e., electricity and steam use) (FutureFuel, 2010). Further discussions of impacts from the emissions of pollutant from the Proposed Project are in Section 3.2.1.2.2.

3.2.1.2   Environmental Consequences

3.2.1.2.1   No Action Alternative

The No Action Alternative is treated in this EA as the "No-Build" Alternative. That is, under the No Action Alternative, DOE would not provide funding for the project, and FutureFuel would not design, install, and operate a commercial plant for the production of high-temperature graphitized precursor anode material for Li-ion batteries. Current emissions would continue unchanged.

With the No Action Alternative, DOE would not fully meet its goal of supporting United States based manufacturing to produce advanced EDV batteries and components. In the absence of DOE funding, industries may be less willing to invest in the advanced technology that would help increase production of these batteries, especially the Li-ion batteries and their components. Without alternative fuel sources for automobiles, the United States would continue its dependence on and consumption of petroleum and other fossil fuels. Consequently, the current trends of increased CO_2 concentrations in the Earth's atmosphere will continue, increasing the effect on climate change. The impact of the No Action Alternative will be minor but will persist over a long period of time.

3.2.1.2.2   Proposed Project

Construction

The FutureFuel Project would involve the retrofit of an existing manufacturing building and would include changes to reactors, piping, and other process equipment located inside the existing building structure (FutureFuel, 2010). FutureFuel also proposes to construct a loading dock for the manufactured materials, the installation of a nitrogen air separation unit package plant on a concrete pad, and the installation of two ASTs for chemical storage. The equipment used for the construct the would intermittently emit quantities of five criteria air pollutants: CO, NO_X, SO_2, PM_{10}, and VOCs. Any new grading or soil disturbance to construct the loading dock, installation of the concrete pad for the nitrogen air separation unit package plant in the utilities area, and the two ASTs would generate fugitive emission.

Fugitive dust, such as dirt stirred up from construction sites, can affect both environmental and public health. The type and severity of the effects depend in large part on the size and nature of the dust particles. The types of effects that can occur to humans include inhalation of fine particles that can then accumulate in the respiratory system causing various respiratory problems including persistent coughs, wheezing, eye irritations, and physical discomfort.

Exhaust emissions from equipment used in construction, coupled with likely fugitive dust emissions, could cause minor, short-term degradation of local air quality. DOE expects the overall impacts to air quality from the construction of the Proposed Project at Batesville, Arkansas would be short-term and minor.

Electric Drive Vehicle Battery and
Component Manufacturing Initiative Project
FutureFuel Chemical Company, Batesville, AR

DOE/EA-1760
Environmental Assessment
August 2010

Operations

FutureFuel no longer operates all of the equipment that is currently in the current Title V permit; however, FutureFuel would continue to maintain ownership of its Title V permit. The equipment and associated emissions for the Proposed Project would replace some of those that have been removed. Although emissions from the proposed plant (see Table 3.2.1-4) would be considerably less than those currently allowed in the Title V permit, FutureFuel would be required to obtain a Title V permit modification from ADEQ (FutureFuel, 2010a).

Because the process design for the Proposed Project is in the initial stages, the actual emissions are currently unknown. However, based on general knowledge and the type of technology that is being proposed for use in the Proposed Project, DOE does not expect that the emissions would increase significantly beyond the current emissions rates. Table 3.2.1-4 provides the expected air emissions from the operations of the proposed process, including material handling operations. Emissions are estimated based on the planned capacity for production of anode material and a 95 percent efficiency of the process control devices. For the proposed process, FutureFuel plans to control emissions using dust collectors and a regenerative thermal oxidizer. The nitrogen air separation unit would not generate any criteria pollutants or HAPs. Although, water vapor and CO_2 would be emitted, CO_2 emissions from the nitrogen air separation unit package plant would be minor or negligible. The existing FutureFuel facility has always complied with its air operating permit, and there are no barriers to impede future compliance.

Table 3.2.1-4. Potential Emissions from the Proposed FutureFuel
Anode Material Production Process

Pollutant	Proposed Operations Potential Emissions Rate (tpy)
PM_{10}	11
SO_2	None expected
VOC	1.25
CO	None expected
NO_X	None expected
Inorganics HAPs	None expected
Organic HAPs	1.25

Source: FutureFuel, 2010a; ADEQ, 2004a

DOE would not be required to demonstrate State Implementation Plan (SIP) conformity because the Proposed Project is in an area that is meeting all NAAQS (40 CFR 93.153(d) (1)). There are no Federal mandatory Class I areas within 62 miles of the Proposed Project location; therefore, a PSD increment and air quality related value analysis for Class I area would not be required. The nearby sensitive receptors would not be affected by direct emissions because the proposed process would be enclosed and emissions would be controlled to limit the amount of pollutants emitted into the atmosphere.

Overall, the Proposed Project operations would have a minor adverse impact on air quality. Although air emissions from the proposed process are measurable, they would result in minimal consequences because of the proposed process's operating control devices that would be used to limit emissions, and emissions would remain below the permit limit.

Carbon Footprint

Arkansas' GHG emissions are higher than nationwide GHG emissions. The State's emissions on a per-capita basis increased by about 10 percent between 1990 and 2005, while United States per-capita emissions declined slightly (2 percent) over this period. On a per-capita basis, Arkansans emitted about 31 metric tons of gross carbon dioxide equivalent (CO_2e) in 2005, which is higher than the national average of about 24 metric tons of

Electric Drive Vehicle Battery and
Component Manufacturing Initiative Project
FutureFuel Chemical Company, Batesville, AR

DOE/EA-1760
Environmental Assessment
August 2010

CO_2e (GCGW, 2008). The principal sources of Arkansas' GHG emissions in 2005 were electricity consumption and transportation, accounting for 32 percent and 26 percent of Arkansas' gross GHG emissions, respectively.

The CO_2 emissions from the Proposed Project are expected to be approximately 9,400 tons per year. However, the FutureFuel facility, which currently exceeds the 25,000 mtpy of CO_2 threshold, would be required to report under the *Final Mandatory Reporting of Greenhouse Gases Rule*.

The manufacture of EDV batteries and components would increase production of EDVs in the United States. EDVs emit no tailpipe pollutants. Therefore, they potentially can provide considerable air quality benefits to targeted regions (DOE, 1999). Overall, there would be beneficial impacts on climate change as the Proposed Project would help the viability of the commercial market for EDVs, thereby reducing the carbon footprint of the transportation sector.

3.2.1.3   Cumulative Impacts

Other than the Proposed Project, no other projects are planned. No reasonably foreseeable actions have been identified that would interact with the Proposed Project to generate cumulative adverse impacts to air quality.

3.2.1.4   Proposed Mitigation Measures

During construction, typical mitigation measures to minimize air quality issues caused by fugitive dust and tailpipe emissions would include the following:

- Require all construction crews and contractors to comply with the State regulations for fugitive dust control during construction.
- Maintain the engines of construction equipment according to manufacturers' specifications.
- Minimize the idling of equipment while the equipment is not in use.
- Implement reasonable measures, such as applying water to exposed surfaces or stockpiles of dirt, when windy or dry conditions promote problematic fugitive dust emissions. Adhering to these best management practices (BMPs) would minimize any fugitive dust emissions. Adhering to mitigation measures and BMPs would reduce the adverse impacts from fugitive dust emissions.

During operations of the Proposed Project, State regulatory authority over air emissions would ensure that the facility continues to meet the requirements of its air operating permit. Because of the control devices used on the equipment and BMPs employed at the facility, actual emissions are to be held well below permitted limits.

3.2.2   Surface Water and Groundwater

3.2.2.1   Affected Environment

Surface Water
The proposed site is located within the Middle White River watershed; United States Geological Survey eight-digit hydrologic unit code (HUC), 11010004. The Middle White River watershed covers approximately 1,476 square miles and contains approximately 2,617 linear miles of streams. Land cover data (2006) indicates the watershed is dominated by forested cover (approximately 69 percent), followed by pasture (approximately 20 percent), urban (approximately 4 percent) and crop (approximately 3 percent) (University of Arkansas, 2010). No portions of the Middle White River are listed on Arkansas's 2010 List of Water Quality Limited Waterbodies (ADEQ, 2010). This portion of the White River is classified for primary contact recreation, raw water source for public, industrial, and agricultural water supplies, propagation of desirable species of fish and other aquatic life, and other compatible uses (ADEQ, 2005). Two tributaries within the 1101004 HUC, Hicks Creek and Greenbriar Creek are both listed as impaired due to pathogen indicators (bacteria), and Greenbriar Creek is also listed as impaired due to low dissolved oxygen (ADEQ, 2010). These tributaries, however, are located upstream of the project site and do not affect the overall attainment status of Middle White River watershed.

Electric Drive Vehicle Battery and
Component Manufacturing Initiative Project
FutureFuel Chemical Company, Batesville, AR

DOE/EA-1760
Environmental Assessment
August 2010

There are no natural surface water features on the project site. A manmade cooling pond (approximately 28 acres) exists on the south side of the project site. Additionally, the White River borders the FutureFuel property, approximately 0.5 miles, to the south of the project site.

The existing facility does obtain process water from the White River through an existing intake, permitted by the U.S. Army Corps of Engineer. The current annual rate of intake is 13,993,531 kilo-gallons (Kgals). Furthermore, the facility discharges wastewater into the White River under National Pollution Discharge Elimination System (NPDES) Permit AR0035386. The permit authorizes the discharge of noncontact cooling water, boiler blowdown, water supply filter backwash, and storm water. The current NPDES permit has limit in terms of discharge temperature (105°F), total carbon content (5 milligrams/liter [mg/l]), oil and grease (15 mg/l) and pH (6 - 9) (ADEQ, 2005). Prior to discharge, wastewater from the facility is first sent through a wastewater treatment plant located onsite for solids removal and pH adjustment. Following treatment in the wastewater treatment plant, treated wastewater is discharged into the White River through a man-made ditch.

Groundwater

The project site is located in the eastern edge of the Ozark Plateau physiographic region province. The Ozark Plateaus aquifer system consists of limestone, dolomite, and sandstone. Aquifers are well-lithified, and permeability is a function of tectonics, diagensis, geochemistry, hydrology, and weathering (USGS, 2010). The Ozark Plateaus aquifer system contains three aquifers, the Springfield Plateau, Ozark, and St. Francois aquifers. The project site is located within the Ozark aquifer which is the thickest and most extensive aquifer within the Ozark Plateaus aquifer system. The aquifer generally is more than 3,000 feet thick in most outcropping localities and serves as a source of water chiefly for agricultural and domestic purposes but supplies some water for municipal and industrial uses (USGS, 2010).

Although the Ozark aquifer is very thick, most of the water withdrawn from the aquifer is obtained from only a few water-yielding zones. In northern Arkansas, the water-yielding characteristics of this formation are poorly understood because it is buried at great depths and, accordingly, are often economically unsuited for development as a water resource. Minor water-yielding zones of the Ozark aquifer are contained within the Jefferson City, the Cotter, and the Powell Dolomites; the upper part of the Everton Formation; the St. Peter Sandstone; and the St. Clair, the Lafferty, and the Clifty Limestones. These strata generally yield less than 50 gallons per minute but are capable of yielding as much as 80 gallons per minute. However, the yield of wells completed in these rocks shows that they are not as permeable as the sandstone beds in the lower part of the aquifer (USGS, 2010).

Dissolved-solids concentrations of water in the Ozark aquifer are, for the most part, less than 400 milligrams per liter throughout northern Arkansas. The largest concentrations of dissolved solids are in eastern Arkansas where the aquifer dips beneath the Coastal Plain (USGS, 2010).

The existing FutureFuel operations do not utilize groundwater resources. Process water is supplied by the White River. Potable water is purchased through the Rock- Moore Water Association. The project site contains 17 groundwater wells that were placed to monitor elevated metal and nitrate concentrations from prior land application of sludge. Six of these wells are actively monitored quarterly. Nitrate concentrations have been detected at levels exceeding the maximum contaminant level of 10 mg/l at a well located south of the land application site (Well A-9). In 1992, at Well A-9, nitrate concentrations exceeded 200 mg/l; concentrations have lowered substantially since that time (the most recent quarterly monitoring results [March-April, 2010] detected nitrate concentrations at 21 mg/l). The overall extent of the contaminant plume has not been delineated (ADEQ, 2004b). Metals concentrations in the groundwater that were elevated above maximum contaminant levels (for beryllium, cadmium, and nickel) were not the result of the applied sludge containing the metals. The metals concentrations resulted from the sludge having a relatively low pH, which ultimately lowered the pH of the downward percolating water causing naturally-occurring metals in the soil to leach out into the groundwater. In 1996, the ADEQ required remedial action, which consisted of applying lime to the sludge land application area to raise the soil pH; lime applications had already been performed for several years previously. The practice

Electric Drive Vehicle Battery and
Component Manufacturing Initiative Project
FutureFuel Chemical Company, Batesville, AR

DOE/EA-1760
Environmental Assessment
August 2010

succeeded in raising the soil pH and, over several years, resulted in less leaching of naturally-occurring metals into the groundwater. Therefore, in 2000, the ADEQ decided that no further action was required with respect to the remediation activities, though groundwater monitoring continues to the present (ADEQ, 2000; FutureFuel, 2010). In 2010, groundwater monitoring resulted in cadmium concentrations ranging from less than 0.004 mg/l to 0.01 mg/l and nickel concentrations ranging from less than 0.01 mg/l to 0.05 mg/l; however, beryllium was not tested for (FutureFuel, 2010b) (also see Section 3.2.4).

3.2.2.2   Environmental Consequences

3.2.2.2.1   No Action Alternative

Under the No Action Alternative, construction and operations would not occur; therefore, no impacts would occur to surface or groundwater resources. The existing facility would continue to operate under their existing NPDES permitting, discharging into the White River. Groundwater would continue to be monitored for metal and nitrate concentrations.

3.2.2.2.2   Proposed Project

Surface Water
Construction

In a letter dated May 12, 2010 (Appendix A), the USFWS recommended that Best Management Practices(BMP) be properly installed and maintained throughout construction to minimize erosion until the site is adequately re-vegetated to prevent soil loss and sedimentation in nearby streams. As the Proposed Project involves the interior retrofitting of an existing building, the potential for erosion and sedimentation would be unlikely and negligible impacts would be anticipated to surface water resources during construction. Construction activities could cause the spill of contaminants (e.g., fuel, oils, antifreeze, etc.) from equipment during construction which would have the potential to runoff into adjacent surface waters (also see USFWS letter in Appendix A). Considering the closest receiving surface water is 0.5 miles to the south of the site, overall adverse impacts during construction would be unlikely. Section 3.2.4.4 discusses the measures which would be taken in the unlikely event of an accidental spill during construction.

Operations

Operations of the Proposed Project would increase the amount of water intake required for operations and would increase the amount of wastewater treated and discharged. Approximately 1,676,109 Kgal annually or an additional 12 percent of cooling water would be withdrawn from the White River. This increase, however, represents a small fraction of the water currently withdrawn from the White River; therefore, adverse impacts would be negligible to surface water resources. Furthermore, no physical changes would be required to the existing intake structure due to the increased uptake of water as the existing structure would be capable of handling increased water demands (FutureFuel, 2010a). Therefore, the current U.S. Army Corps of Engineers permitted intake structure would not need to be modified. Wastewater (i.e., non-contact cooling water, process water, and sanitary water) discharge into the White River would also increase by approximately 12 percent, reflective of the increased water usage. This increase, however, would not be anticipated to cause a significant adverse affect to the water quality within the White River. The discharges from the Proposed Project would be similar in nature to wastewater produced by other existing operations and would, therefore, not be expected to change the chemical composition or thermal characteristics of current discharges. Current NPDES Permit AR0035386 discharge limits would apply; no modification would be required as chemical composition and thermal characteristics would remain similar to existing discharges permitted. FutureFuel would continue to adhere to the general, monitoring, and reporting requirements contained within the existing NPDES Permit AR0035386. Operations also have the potential to indirectly impact water quality through the spill of contaminants (e.g., fuel, oils, antifreeze, etc.) from vehicles during operations. As part of the Proposed Project, however, an oil water separator would be added to the area adjacent to the new loading area, minimizing the potential for adverse impacts. Overall impacts to surface waters from the Proposed Project would, therefore, be minor.

Electric Drive Vehicle Battery and
Component Manufacturing Initiative Project
FutureFuel Chemical Company, Batesville, AR

DOE/EA-1760
Environmental Assessment
August 2010

Groundwater
Construction

FutureFuel would develop BMPs to guide the avoidance, minimization, and response to pollutant spills that could affect groundwater during construction. In addition, the existing facility operates under a Spill Prevention, Control, and Countermeasures (SPCC) Plan to minimize the potential for damaging spills to take place. It is possible that an accidental release of toxic materials to groundwater could happen; however, through adherence to appropriate BMPs and the SPCC Plan, the potential for groundwater contamination to occur during construction would be minor.

Construction activities would not be expected to have any impacts with respect to the existing groundwater contamination. There are no groundwater wells in the areas of proposed construction. The extent of the contaminant plume has not been delineated; thus, it is currently unknown if it underlies the proposed construction areas. No deep digging or trenching would be expected that could create pathways to the groundwater.

Operations

No groundwater withdrawals are proposed; therefore, no impacts on groundwater levels would occur. As stated above under 'Construction", the existing facility operates under an SPCC Plan, which would apply to the proposed operations as well. In addition, Standard Operating Procedures and BMPs would be developed and adhered to for the safe handling of toxic materials and procedures to follow in the event of an accidental spill. Thus, the potential for groundwater contamination to occur during operations would be minor. No activities are proposed that would be expected to cause an impact with respect to the existing onsite groundwater contamination.

3.2.2.3   Cumulative Impacts

Although approximately 27 percent of the Middle White River watershed has been converted to pasture, urban and cropland, the overall water quality of the Middle White River remains intact; no portions of the Middle White River are listed on Arkansas's 2010 List of Water Quality Limited Waterbodies. The Proposed Project would not contribute to changes in land cover or discharge limits that would be anticipated to adversely and cumulative impact water quality of the White River. Furthermore, past use of the site has resulted in groundwater contamination (elevated metal and nitrate concentrations). The contamination plume would continue to be monitored and remediated, and the Proposed Project is not anticipated to contribute to groundwater impacts, therefore, no cumulative adverse impacts on groundwater levels would occur.

3.2.2.4   Proposed Mitigation Measures

No mitigation measures would be required for surface water and groundwater.

3.2.3   Transportation and Traffic

3.2.3.1   Affected Environment

The proposed site is an industrial facility located approximately 8 miles southeast of Batesville, Arkansas. The property consists of approximately 400 acres of developed land located on a campus of over 2,200 acres. The property is bounded by the White River to the south, Russell Ferry Road to the west, Gap Road to the north, and Waldrip Road to the east. The area surrounding the FutureFuel property is characterized by wooded areas with dispersed residential properties.

The entrance to the site is on Gap Road. Gap Road intersects State Highway 69 (Harrison Street) approximately 1.6 miles to the east of the site, and also intersects State Highway 69 approximately 6 miles to the west of the site passing through more residential areas. Typically, the FutureFuel truck traffic travels on Gap Road in the easterly direction to State Highway 69, the nearest accessible major arterial road. State Highway 69 travels west to intersect Highway 167, which can be traveled south toward Little Rock, Arkansas; and State Highway 69 travels

Electric Drive Vehicle Battery and
Component Manufacturing Initiative Project
FutureFuel Chemical Company, Batesville, AR

DOE/EA-1760
Environmental Assessment
August 2010

east to Newport, Arkansas, with access to State Highway 14, which leads toward Memphis, Tennessee (EPA, 2010a; FutureFuel, 2010a). Gap Road has a current average daily traffic count of 860 vehicles; and State Highway 69 has a current average daily traffic count of approximately 5,500 vehicles between the eastern and western intersections with Gap Road (AHTD, 2010). State Highway 69 is currently being improved with road widening and new signals, and is near completion. There are various sparsely traveled rural roads directly surrounding the property, providing access to the few surrounding residences.

3.2.3.2   Environmental Consequences

3.2.3.2.1   No Action Alternative

Under the No Action Alternative, construction and operations would not occur, therefore, no impacts would occur to transportation and traffic.

3.2.3.2.2   Proposed Project

Construction
Short-term but measurable adverse impacts to traffic are expected during the construction phase of the Proposed Project. It is anticipated that approximately 100 construction workers would access the site during this period. Construction-related vehicles would add to existing local traffic and would potentially cause minor congestion, higher traffic noise, and increased vehicle emissions along the routes. Construction worker traffic would occur primarily at the beginning and ending of the workday. The roads most impacted would be Gap Road and State Highway 69, which would have adequate capacity to handle the additional traffic, particularly after the widening of State Highway 69 is completed. Construction impacts to existing transportation resources would be minor, temporary, and localized. No aspect of the construction phase is anticipated to force temporary road closures or detours. The construction would be expected to last for approximately 13 months.

Operations
The Proposed Project would be expected to result in a minor long-term increase in truck and personal-vehicle traffic. The project would require an increase of approximately 15 trucks per week (3 per day) in and out of the property during operations. This additional truck traffic would amount to at most an approximate 15 percent increase in truck traffic from existing conditions, and would therefore generate a minor impact on traffic conditions. The additional truck trips would use the established truck routes currently in place. The additional truck trips could adequately be accommodated within the existing roadway and intersection networks, particularly after improvements to State Highway 69 are completed.

The Proposed Project would generate an increase in privately-owned vehicle traffic due to the hiring of approximately 33 additional permanent employees. The workers would be split among operation shifts, thus reducing the impact on traffic. The additional vehicle traffic would constitute an approximate 4 percent increase in the current average daily traffic count on Gap Road, and less than 1 percent of an increase on State Highway 69. This small increase in traffic would have only a minor impact on the surrounding community.

3.2.3.3   Cumulative Impacts

Other than the Proposed Project, no other projects are planned. No reasonably foreseeable traffic-related actions have been identified that would interact with the Proposed Project to generate cumulative adverse impacts to transportation and traffic.

3.2.3.4   Proposed Mitigation Measures

No mitigation measures would be required for transportation and traffic.

Electric Drive Vehicle Battery and
Component Manufacturing Initiative Project
FutureFuel Chemical Company, Batesville, AR

DOE/EA-1760
Environmental Assessment
August 2010

3.2.4   Solid and Hazardous Waste

3.2.4.1   Affected Environment

The Emergency Planning and Community Right-To-Know Act, also known as Superfund Amendments and Reauthorization Act (SARA) Title III requires manufacturing facilities to submit an annual toxic chemical release report if they manufacture, process, or use specified chemicals in amounts greater than threshold quantities. This report, commonly known as Form R, covers releases and transfers of toxic chemicals to various facilities and environmental media, and allows EPA to compile the national Toxic Release Inventory database. The existing FutureFuel facility has submitted Form Rs for approximately 25 materials, depending on usage during a particular reporting year. The Toxic Release Inventory materials used in the highest quantity at the FutureFuel facility over the past 5 years include methanol, benzene, cumene, toluene, chlorobenzene, phenol, n-hexane, xylene, hydrochloric acid, and chlorine (FutureFuel, 2010a).

The facility is located in EPA Region 6 and operates as a large-quantity generator of hazardous waste (EPA Identification number ARD089234884), which means the facility generates more than 2,200 pounds or more of hazardous waste or more than 2.2 pounds of acute hazardous waste per calendar month. Based on FutureFuel's Annual Hazardous Waste Report for 2009, the predominant hazardous wastes generated include spent organic process waste, solvents, aqueous waste, acids, paint-related waste (FutureFuel, 2010c). The Arkansas Department of Environmental Quality (ADEQ) implements Arkansas' hazardous waste management and solid waste programs and enforces the hazardous and non-hazardous waste management rules and has delegation of the Federal Resource Conservation and Recovery Act (RCRA) hazardous waste management program from EPA. State and Federal hazardous waste management regulations and requirements are incorporated in to Arkansas Pollution Control and Ecology Commission Regulation 23.

Approximately 900,000 pounds of non-hazardous solid waste was transported offsite for recycling or disposal in 2009 (FutureFuel, 2010a). The facility generated approximately 66 million pounds of hazardous waste in 2009; 1 million pounds was shipped offsite; 65 million pounds were treated onsite and was either used as a beneficial fuel for the onsite boilers or was incinerated in the onsite incinerator (FutureFuel, 2010c).

The FutureFuel facility is a permitted transport, storage, and treatment facility (RCRA Permit 11H-RN1). The facility generates hazardous waste that is stored in 11 hazardous waste management tanks and used as supplemental fuel in one of the three coal-fired boilers or destroyed in the onsite incinerator. Some of what is burned in the incinerator is organic waste (e.g., spent solvents, organic process wastes), but the majority is an aqueous waste stream containing some organic and some salt compounds (ADEQ, 2008). The facility is permitted to accept hazardous waste from an offsite source, provided the amount of such waste does not exceed 5 percent of the Permittee's annual operating capacity. The RCRA storage tanks are located on reinforced concrete foundation slabs with either 2 or 3 foot high perimeter concrete walls with adequate containment to contain the capacity of the largest tank and a 25-year, 24-hour rainfall event (ADEQ, 2008).

A RCRA Facility Assessment was performed in 1988, which recommended 19 solid waste management units (SWMUs) undergo further investigation. Eastman SE, Inc. (Eastman) (former owner of the FutureFuel property) conducted a RCRA Facility Investigation (RFI) of the 19 SWMUs and issued a Final RFI Report on August 31, 1993. The RFI investigation of the 19 SWMUs found contamination at two of the SWMUs. One SWMU, the Spray Irrigation Area, had beryllium, cadmium, and nickel in concentrations above background levels and maximum contaminant levels (MCLs) in the shallow flow zone groundwater immediately down gradient of the Spray Irrigation Area. Cobalt and zinc were also detected above background levels down gradient of the Spray Irrigation Area. At the second SWMU, the Wastewater Basins Area, barium and cobalt were detected down gradient at concentrations above background in the shallow flow zone groundwater (ADEQ, 2008).

Based on the results of the RFI, Eastman was required to monitor the groundwater down gradient of the Wastewater Basins Area, but no remediation was required. Eastman was, however, required to propose

Electric Drive Vehicle Battery and
Component Manufacturing Initiative Project
FutureFuel Chemical Company, Batesville, AR

DOE/EA-1760
Environmental Assessment
August 2010

remediation for the shallow groundwater down gradient of the Spray Irrigation Area. The initial Remedial Action Decision Document (RADD) for Corrective Action for the Spray Irrigation Area was issued on June 27, 1996. The remediation selected was aggressive liming to raise the Spray Irrigation Area soil pH to prevent the leaching of naturally-occurring metals present in the soil. A final RADD for Corrective Action was issued in October 2000. The Final RADD required no further action under RCRA for the two SWMUs (Spray Irrigation Area and Wastewater Basins Area). Regulation of the two SWMUs was transferred from ADEQ's RCRA Division to the ADEQ Water Division. Therefore, liming of the Spray Irrigation Area and groundwater monitoring is currently regulated under the facility's NPDES permit (permit number AR0035386) (ADEQ, 2008; FutureFuel, 2010a). Land application of sludge (generated from the onsite wastewater treatment plant) in the Spray Irrigation Area is also permitted under FutureFuel's NPDES permit.

Quarterly groundwater monitoring is performed and annual reports are submitted to the ADEQ. Groundwater samples are analyzed for pH, nitrates, Pb, cadmium, nickel, copper, and zinc in accordance with FutureFuel's NPDES permit. Nitrate concentrations have been detected at levels exceeding the maximum contaminant level of 10 mg/l at a well located south of the land application site (Well A-9). In 1992, at Well A-9, nitrate concentrations exceeded 200 mg/l; concentrations have lowered substantially since that time (in 2004 nitrate concentrations ranged from 40 to 50 mg/l); the most recent quarterly monitoring results (March-April, 2010) detected nitrate concentrations from Well A-9 at 21 mg/l. Concentrations of metals in groundwater have either been below the detection limit or were not detected at significant levels (highest detected concentration in most recent groundwater sampling was 0.12 mg/l for copper) (FutureFuel, 2010a).

The facility has a SPCC Plan in place that addresses the quantity, storage, and handling of oil in accordance with 40 CFR 112. Table 3.2.4-1 lists the 15 ASTs at the facility used to store oil. In addition, the facility stores hydraulic oil in operating equipment with capacities ranging from 70 gallons to 215 gallons; the oil-containing equipment and associated hydraulic oil tanks are located inside buildings or equipped with containment (FutureFuel, 2009).

Table 3.2.4-1. Existing Aboveground Storage Tanks at the FutureFuel Facility

Material Stored	Capacity (Gallons)	Secondary Containment	Overfill Protection
Biodiesel	12,500	Concrete containment	High level liquid alarm (Alarm), high liquid level pump cutoff (Cutoff)
Biodiesel	47,000	Concrete containment	High level liquid alarm (Alarm), high liquid level pump cutoff (Cutoff)
Crude Biodiesel	47,000	Concrete containment	High level liquid alarm (Alarm), high liquid level pump cutoff (Cutoff)
Animal Fat	47,000	Concrete containment	High level liquid alarm (Alarm), high liquid level pump cutoff (Cutoff)
Animal Fat	47,000	Concrete containment	High level liquid alarm (Alarm), high liquid level pump cutoff (Cutoff)
Biodiesel	100	Concrete containment	Person present at all times during transfer
Biodiesel	100	Concrete containment	Person present at all times during transfer
Diesel	500	Metal containment	Person present at all times during transfer
Diesel	500	Metal containment	Person present at all times during transfer
Biodiesel or Raw Oil	370,000	Earthen containment	High level liquid alarm (Alarm), high liquid level pump cutoff (Cutoff)
Biodiesel or Raw Oil	370,000	Earthen containment	High level liquid alarm (Alarm), high liquid level pump cutoff (Cutoff)

Electric Drive Vehicle Battery and
Component Manufacturing Initiative Project
FutureFuel Chemical Company, Batesville, AR

DOE/EA-1760
Environmental Assessment
August 2010

Table 3.2.4-1. Existing Aboveground Storage Tanks at the FutureFuel Facility (continued)

Material Stored	Capacity (Gallons)	Secondary Containment	Overfill Protection
Biodiesel or Raw Oil	370,000	Earthen containment	High level liquid alarm (Alarm), high liquid level pump cutoff (Cutoff)
Raw Oil	4,000,000	Earthen containment	High level liquid level alarm (Alarm)
Biodiesel or Raw Oil	4,000,000	Earthen containment	High level liquid alarm (Alarm), high liquid level pump cutoff (Cutoff)
Biodiesel or Raw Oil	4,000,000	Earthen containment	High level liquid alarm (Alarm), high liquid level pump cutoff (Cutoff)
B20 Biodiesel	12,000	Double-walled tank	High liquid level pump cutoff (Cutoff)

Source: FutureFuel, 2009a.

The site is not listed on the EPA's National Priority List, which designates high-priority cleanup sites under the Comprehensive Environmental Response Compensation and Liability Act, more commonly known as the Superfund Program. There is no known polychlorinated biphenyl-containing equipment onsite. There are areas in the existing facility where asbestos-containing material and Pb-based paint are reported to be present.

3.2.4.2 Environmental Consequences

3.2.4.2.1 No Action Alternative

Under the No Action Alternative, the facility would continue its current operations and would generate the same types and quantities of hazardous and non-hazardous wastes. Wastes would continue to be collected for energy recovery in three of its boilers or be incinerated in the onsite incinerator in accordance with its RCRA permit and with all applicable Federal, State and local regulations. The facility would continue to monitoring groundwater and would continue to land apply sludge from its wastewater treatment plant in accordance with its NPDES permit.

3.2.4.2.2 Proposed Project

Construction

The Proposed Project would be located primarily within an existing building at the FutureFuel facility. New construction would include a loading dock, a concrete pad for the nitrogen air separation unit package plant, and two, 35,000-gallon ASTs to store xylene and pitch. The new loading dock, concrete pad, and ASTs would be constructed on previously disturbed land. Construction is likely to generate a small quantity of solid waste from building materials; no hazardous waste would be expected to be generated during construction. The construction waste materials could be landfilled off site at a permitted solid waste landfill. Solid waste and sanitary waste generated during construction activities would be limited to common construction-related waste streams. In-state or out-of-state landfills or recycling facilities would have the capability and capacity to accept these wastes. No demolition of structures would be required.

Solid waste and sanitary waste generated during construction would be limited to common construction-related waste streams. In state or out-of-state landfills or recycling facilities would have the capability and capacity to accept these wastes. There are no known instances of contamination in the areas where project activities would occur. No impact from construction to solid and hazardous waste management would occur.

Electric Drive Vehicle Battery and
Component Manufacturing Initiative Project
FutureFuel Chemical Company, Batesville, AR

DOE/EA-1760
Environmental Assessment
August 2010

Operations

Proposed operations at the new plant would increase the materials currently used, and would introduce two new materials (coke and pitch) (see Table 3.2.4-2). FutureFuel estimates an increase in the use of xylene by 6.6 million pounds per year above what is currently used. A 35,000-gallon AST of xylene and a 35,000-gallon of pitch would be added to the facility. Nonhazardous waste would be sent offsite for recycling or to be landfilled. Hazardous waste generated from the Proposed Project would primarily be spent solvents that would be directed to the onsite hazardous waste incinerator/coal units for energy recovery. An increase of 13.1 million pounds per year of hazardous waste comprised of pitch and xylene would be generated and incinerated as beneficial fuel onsite.

Table 3.2.4-2 Projected Material Usage and Waste Generated
for Proposed Project

Material	Annual Usage	Units
Xylene	6,570,000	Pounds
Coke	9,490,000	Pounds
Pitch	7,119,000	Pounds
Product	10,000,000	Pounds
Nonhazardous solid waste municipal	30,000	Pounds
Nonhazardous solid waste off-site	39,469	Pounds
Liquid hazardous waste (pitch and xylene)	13,100,000	Pounds

FutureFuel, 2010a

As a large-quantity generator of hazardous waste, the facility is required to have a Preparedness and Prevention Program and a RCRA Contingency Plan in accordance with 40 CFR 262.34(a)(4) and to train its employees on the safe and proper handling of hazardous waste. These existing plans and training would be expanded to include the safe handling of coke and pitch and the newly constructed loading dock, nitrogen air separation unit package plant, and ASTs. The plans would include an evaluation of alternatives to eliminate, reduce, or minimize the amounts of hazardous materials used and hazardous wastes generated and procedures to take in the event of a release. The facility must also adhere to conditions of its RCRA Permit to ensure the proper handling and disposal of hazardous wastes burned for beneficial reuse in its boilers or incinerator. In addition, the facility would continue to meet the requirements under its NPDES permit for monitoring of groundwater and for land application of sludge from its wastewater treatment plant.

Two new 35,000-gallon ASTs to store xylene and petroleum pitch would be installed on a concrete pad with vertical concrete containment walls. The containment would be equipped with a drain valve that would be kept closed, but could be opened to drain rainwater after visual observation shows no signs of oil. The nitrogen air separator unit package plant would be installed on a new concrete pad and would include two compressors and air and nitrogen surge tanks. The facility has an SPCC Plan in place that would be modified to include the additional tanks to be added to the facility. Because the ASTs to store xylene and petroleum pitch would be equipped with secondary containment and FutureFuel has an SPCC Plan and emergency procedures in place to address an accidental release, the potential for impact to solid and hazardous waste from the new ASTs would be minor. The nitrogen and air tanks associated with the air separator unit package plant would not be expected to have an impact.

Electric Drive Vehicle Battery and
Component Manufacturing Initiative Project
FutureFuel Chemical Company, Batesville, AR

DOE/EA-1760
Environmental Assessment
August 2010

3.2.4.3 Cumulative Impacts

Other than the Proposed Project, no other projects are planned. Therefore, no reasonably foreseeable actions have been identified that would interact with the Proposed Project to generate cumulative adverse impacts.

3.2.4.4 Proposed Mitigation Measures

During construction, preventative measures such as establishing contained storage areas, and controlling the flow of construction equipment and personnel would reduce the potential for a release to occur. In the event that a release occurs, immediate action would be taken to contain and clean up the released material in accordance with Federal, State, and local regulations.

During operations, adoption of safety and emergency response plans to include the new processes and the safe handling and storage of chemicals at the site, as well as employee training, would limit the potential for a release at the facility.

3.2.5 Human Health and Safety

3.2.5.1 Affected Environment

In accordance with 40 CFR Part 68, an owner or operator of a stationary source that has more than a threshold quantity of a regulated substance in a process is required to prepare a Risk Management Plan (RMP). The FutureFuel facility has a RMP in place that is submitted to the EPA in accordance with 40 CFR Part 68. FutureFuel's RMP includes regulated flammables (proprietary) and propylene. In addition, the facility uses chlorine, crotonaldehyde, oleum (20 percent and 30 percent), anhydrous hydrogen chloride, formaldehyde, phosphorus oxychloride, phosphorus trichloride, and vinyl acetate monomer, which are RMP-regulated toxic substances. There have been no injuries involving a RPM chemical; there have been zero incidents with off-site effects (FutureFuel, 2009b). In accordance with the regulations set forth in 40 CFR Part 68, FutureFuel has an Accidental Release Prevention and Emergency Response Program in place that includes its RMP, emergency response and mitigation if an accidental release should occur, and notification to public officials in the event of an emergency. The facility must also perform regular hazard assessments for chemicals included in its RMP.

FutureFuel has trained employees knowledgeable of the materials used at the facility. Employees are trained on the hazards of handling materials, appropriate personal protective equipment for each material and chemical-specific emergency response procedures. Training includes procedures for the safe handling to manufacture, process, store, and transport the materials as well as actions to follow in the event of a release in a manner that minimizes the impact on the health and safety of workers, the community and the environment. The facility conducts periodic health assessments and industrial hygiene monitoring to evaluate and minimize the potential for exposure to employees. (FutureFuel, 2009b). The potential for exposure to onsite chemicals is primarily contained within buildings and secured areas of the property. The facility is fenced with controlled access with a gate and a guard is present during daytime hours, and a patrolling guard is present 24 hours a day, 365 days a year.

FutureFuel has multiple systems in place that are designed to backup another system to prevent a release from the facility. The first layer involves accident prevention by identifying and reducing risks during the design and before startup of new manufacturing processes. The second layer involves operating and maintaining equipment and processes in a manner that reduces risks and minimizes incidents. The third layer involves maintaining the capability to respond to and control incidents in a timely manner.

Electric Drive Vehicle Battery and
Component Manufacturing Initiative Project
FutureFuel Chemical Company, Batesville, AR

DOE/EA-1760
Environmental Assessment
August 2010

3.2.5.2   Environmental Consequences

3.2.5.2.1   No Action Alternative

Under the No Action Alternative, the facility would continue its current operations and would generate the same types and quantities of hazardous and non-hazardous wastes. Wastes would continue to be collected and either used as beneficial fuel in one of its boilers or incinerated in the onsite incinerator in accordance with its RCRA Permit and all applicable Federal, State, and local regulations. The facility would continue to monitoring groundwater and would continue to land apply sludge from its wastewater treatment plant in accordance with its NPDES permit.

3.2.5.2.2   Proposed Project

Construction

The Proposed Project would involve new construction of a loading dock, a concrete pad, and two ASTs on land currently used for industrial purposes of graded areas within the fenced and guarded area of the FutureFuel facility. Construction workers would be trained to follow safety standards applicable to the construction site hazards to ensure the health and safety of workers, particularly the hazards and emergency response associated with RMP-regulated materials. No impact related to health and safety would occur under the Proposed Project from construction of the plant.

Operations

Materials to be used and stored at the plant, as described in Section 3.2.4.2, would be similar to what is currently used at the plant. However, the Proposed Project would introduce coke and pitch to its operations and would increase the use of xylene. Pitch and xylene would be stored in two new 35,000-gallon ASTs, one to store xylene and one to store pitch. As previously described, the facility has a RMP in place. The risk for a release from the Proposed Project would not increase the potential for exposure to offsite receptors from what currently exists. FutureFuel would have to revise its Emergency Response and Safety Plans to incorporate the new operations, including the loading dock, nitrogen air separation unit package plant, and two new ASTs.

The Health and Safety Plans in place address potential hazards associated with handling materials as well as the personal protective equipment necessary when handling the materials, emergency response actions to be followed in the event of a release, and spill containment and control if a spill of a liquid material should occur. The facility's site security outlines procedures to follow to prevent unauthorized access to the property.

Because materials and resulting wastes would be similar to what is currently used and generated, the potential risk of exposure would be greatest for FutureFuel employees, who would be trained in proper safety procedures. The risk of exposure to the general population would be similar to what currently exists. The health and safety risks associated with onsite processes would be addressed in procedures developed to guide the safe handling of materials and waste. The principal hazards associated with plant operations (exposure to from chemical handling and equipment operation) would be contained within buildings and secure areas of the property. The facility's existing Safety Plan would be modified to address any new safety hazards and would ensure that appropriate training on proper procedures and safety would be provided to protect workers. With appropriate safety procedures in place and the use of personal protective equipment, the potential for an impact to the health and safety of workers would be minor.

Because critical hourly or daily functions of strategic importance to the national economy are not reliant on plant operations, the FutureFuel facility is not considered a potential target for intentional destructive acts. Although the supply of produced compounds could be interrupted temporarily by a destructive act, the interruption would be relatively brief and would not be expected to have lasting effects on the economy. The plant is secured against public access and buffered by distance from residential areas. The potential for impacts of an intentional destructive act on human health and safety would be reduced through implementation of procedures in the Safety Plan.

Electric Drive Vehicle Battery and
Component Manufacturing Initiative Project
FutureFuel Chemical Company, Batesville, AR

DOE/EA-1760
Environmental Assessment
August 2010

3.2.5.3 Cumulative Impacts

Other than the Proposed Project, no other projects are planned. Therefore, no foreseeable actions have been identified that would interact with the Proposed Project to generate cumulative adverse impacts to human health and safety.

3.2.5.4 Proposed Mitigation Measures

During construction, safety measures such as establishing contained storage areas, and controlling the movement of construction equipment and personnel would reduce the potential for an accident to occur. Safety awareness training is required for construction workers on the chemical hazards present at the site and emergency procedures to follow in the event of an accidental release. Additionally, Section 3.2.1.4 identifies proposed mitigation measures to minimize human health and safety impacts to air quality caused by fugitive dust and tailpipe emissions.

During operations, mitigation measures would include appropriate training of all employees in the safe handling and storage of chemicals onsite that would be used for the Proposed Project.

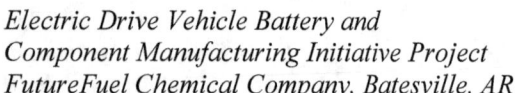

Electric Drive Vehicle Battery and
Component Manufacturing Initiative Project
FutureFuel Chemical Company, Batesville, AR

DOE/EA-1760
Environmental Assessment
August 2010

This page intentionally left blank.

Electric Drive Vehicle Battery and
Component Manufacturing Initiative Project
FutureFuel Chemical Company, Batesville, AR

DOE/EA-1760
Environmental Assessment
August 2010

4.0   REFERENCES

40 CFR 50 "National Primary and Secondary Ambient Air Quality Standards" U.S. Environmental Protection Agency, Code of Federal Regulations.

40 CFR 51.166. "Requirements for Preparation, Adoption and Submittal of Implementation Plans: Prevention of Significant Deterioration of Air Quality." U.S. Environmental Protection Agency, Code of Federal Regulations.

40 CFR 52.21(c). "Prevention of Significant Deterioration of Air Quality: Ambient air increments." U.S. Environmental Protection Agency, Code of Federal Regulations.

40 CFR 52.21. "Prevention of Significant Deterioration of Air Quality." U.S. Environmental Protection Agency, Code of Federal Regulations.

40 CFR 93. "Determining Conformity of Federal Actions to State or Federal Implementation Plans." U.S. Environmental Protection Agency, Code of Federal Regulations.

Arkansas Department of Environmental Quality (ADEQ). 2000. *Arkansas Eastman Final Revised Remedial Action Decision Document Class 3 Permit Modification.* Permit 11H-M005. October 19, 2000.

ADEQ. 2004a. ADEQ Operating Air Permit. Issued January 20, 2004. Expired January 19, 2009.

ADEQ. 2004b. *The Arkansas Department of Environmental Quality's Proposed Findings of Fact.* Docket No. 03-007-P. By Daniel D. Etzkorn (ADEQ). May 7, 2004.

ADEQ. 2005. Authorization to Discharge under the National Pollutant Discharge Elimination System and the Arkansas Waster and Air Pollution Control Act. Permit number: AR0035386.

ADEQ. 2008. RCRA Permit 11H-RN1, Class 2 Permit Modification Request. January 4, 2008.

ADEQ. 2010. Arkansas Watershed Information System - 8-Digit: 11010004. http://watersheds.cast.uark.edu/viewhuc.php?hucid=11010004 Site Accessed April 22, 2010.

Arkansas Governor's Commission on Global Warming (GCGW), 2008. Final GCGW Report, October 2008

Arkansas State Highway and Transportation Department (AHTD), 2010. 2009 Annual Average Daily Traffic Estimates. Independence County. Accessed April 30, 2010 at http://www.arkansashighways.com/planning_research/technical_services/TrafficCountyMaps/2009ADT/counties/INDEPENDENCE.pdf

DOE. 1999. Department of Energy, GREET 1.5 Transportation Fuel-Cycle Mode. Accessed on November 7, 2009 at the U.S. Department of Energy - Energy Efficiency and Renewable Energy, Alternative Fuels and Advanced Vehicles Data Center: http://www.afdc.energy.gov/afdc/vehicles/emissions_electricity.html (last updated August 6, 2009).

Entergy Power. 2010. About Us. http://www.entergy.com/about_entergy/. Accessed: April 22, 2010.

EPA. 2010a. NEPAssist accessed April 30, 2010, at http://epamap9.epa.gov/nepave/nepamap.aspx?action=openses&p_nepaid=13493720100429FCARE

EPA. 2010b. National Ambient Air Quality Standards (NAAQS). Accessed April 30, 2010 at http://epa.gov/air/criteria.html (last updated April 16, 2010).

EPA, 2010c. The Green Book Nonattainment Areas for Criteria Pollutants. Accessed April 30, 2010 at http://www.epa.gov/oar/oaqps/greenbk/index.html (last updated January 6, 2010)

Electric Drive Vehicle Battery and
Component Manufacturing Initiative Project
FutureFuel Chemical Company, Batesville, AR

DOE/EA-1760
Environmental Assessment
August 2010

EPA, 2010d, *2008 Ground-level Ozone Standards — Region 6 Recommendations and EPA Responses* Accessed April 30, 2010 at http://www.epa.gov/ozonedesignations/2008standards/rec/letters/06_AR_rec.pdf (letter dated March 10, 2009)

Federal Emergency Management Agency (FEMA). 2010. Flood Insurance Rate Map, Independence County and Incorporated Areas, Panel 375 of 550. Map Number 05063C0375D. March 17, 2010.

FutureFuel. 2009a. Spill Prevention Control and Countermeasure Plan. [confidential]

FutureFuel. 2009b. FutureFuel Risk Management Plan, Executive Summary. [confidential]

FutureFuel. 2010a. Information Provided in Support of Application to Department of Energy. [confidential]

FutureFuel. 2010b. *2010 Spray Irrigation Report, Permit# AR0035386, Ground Water Monitoring.* Analyses performed by American Interplex Corporation.

FutureFuel. 2010c. FutureFuel Hazardous Waste Report for 2009.

Liu and Liptak. 1997. Environmental Engineers' Handbook. Second Edition. Lewis Publishers.

National Park Service (NPS). 2009a. National Park Service, Class I Area Location. Accessed November 2, 2009 at http://www.nature.nps.gov/air/Maps/classILoc.cfm (last updated December 16, 2007)

NPS, 2009b. National Park Service, Permit Application, PSD Overview. Accessed November 2, 2009 at http://www.nature.nps.gov/air/permits/index.cfm (last updated March 28, 2006)

Natural Resource Conservation Service (NRCS). 2008. Independence County Arkansas Soil Survey. Version 9, Nov 28, 2008.

Rock-Moore Water Association. 2010. Communication by phone on April 20, 2010.

United States Fish and Wildlife Service (USFWS). 2010. Wetlands Mapper. Map center: 35° 43' 11" N, 91° 31' 39" W. http://wetlandsfws.er.usgs.gov/imf/imf.jsp?site=NWI_CONUS. Site Accessed March 22, 2010.

United States Geological Survey (USGS). 2010. GroundWater Atlas of the United States, Arkansas, Louisiana, Mississippi HA 730-F; Ozark Plateaus Aquifer System. http://pubs.usgs.gov/ha/ha730/ch_f/F-text6.html Site Accessed April 22, 2010.

University of Arkansas. 2010. State of Arkansas 2010 List of Impaired Waterbodies. Prepared pursuant to Section 305(b) and 303(d) of the of the Federal Water Pollution Control Act.

Electric Drive Vehicle Battery and
Component Manufacturing Initiative Project
FutureFuel Chemical Company, Batesville, AR

DOE/EA-1760
Environmental Assessment
August 2010

5.0 LIST OF PREPARERS

Department of Energy	
John Tabacchi	Project Manager
Pierina Fayish	NEPA Document Manager
William Gwilliam	NEPA Document Manager

FutureFuel	
Jim Ross	Manager, Environmental Affairs
Gary McChesney	Chief Technology Officer
Dan Walden	Technical Associate

PHE		
Analyst	**Responsibilites**	**Degrees and Experience**
Anthony Becker	Technical Writer: Surface Water, Groundwater	M.S., Biology B.S., Biology 5 years experience, 5 years NEPA experience
Frederick Carey, P.E.	Senior Engineer, QA/QC	M.S., Environmental Engineering B.S., Civil Engineering 17 years experience, 17 years NEPA experience
Austina Casey	Technical Writer: Air Quality and Climate	M.S., Environmental Science and Policy B.S., Chemistry 18 years experience, 6 years NEPA experience
Brandon Campion	Technical Writer: Utilities and Energy Use	B.S., Environmental Policy and Planning 2 years NEPA experience
Angela Drum	Senior Word Processor	10 years experience, 5 years NEPA experience
Joseph Grieshaber	QA/QC	M.B.A., Finance M.S., Biology B.S., Biology 34 years experience, 21 years NEPA experience
Robin Griffin	Assistant Project Manager, Technical Writer: Cultural Resources	M.S., Environmental Management B.A., English Composition 17 years experience, 15 years NEPA experience
Jamie Martin-McNaughton	Sharepoint Administrator	B.S., Geology-Biology 7 years experience, 5 years NEPA experience
Robert Naumann	Technical Writer: Geology and Soils, Wetlands and Floodplains, Vegetation and Wildlife	B.S., Natural Resources M.S., Environmental Science 11 years experience, 11 years NEPA experience
Deborah Shinkle	GIS Specialist	B.A., Environmental Studies 6 years experience, 5 years NEPA experience
Rachel Spangenberg	Technical Writer: Materials and Waste Management	B.S., Biology 20 years experience, 15 years NEPA experience
Debra Walker	Project Manager	B.S., Biology 33 years experience, 20 years NEPA experience
Andrea Wilkes	Technical Writer: Noise, Traffic and Transportation	M.A., Science Writing B.S., Civil and Environmental Engineering B.S., English Literature 24 years experience, 2 years NEPA experience
Julia Norris	Technical Writer: Land Use, Environmental Justice, Visual Resources, and Socioeconomics	B.S., Environmental Conservation 10 years experience, 8 years NEPA experience

Electric Drive Vehicle Battery and
Component Manufacturing Initiative Project
FutureFuel Chemical Company, Batesville, AR

DOE/EA-1760
Environmental Assessment
August 2010

This page intentionally left blank.

Electric Drive Vehicle Battery and
Component Manufacturing Initiative Project
FutureFuel Chemical Company, Batesville, AR

DOE/EA-1760
Environmental Assessment
August 2010

6.0   DISTRIBUTION LIST

Mr. John Bailey, P.E.
Technical Assistance Manager
Water Division
Arkansas Department of Environmental Quality
5301 Northshore Drive
North Little Rock, AR 72118-5317

Honorable Mike Beebe
Governor of Arkansas
State Capitol Room 250
Little Rock, AR 72201

Mr. Tracy L. Copeland
Manager, Arkansas State Clearinghouse
Office of Intergovernmental Services
P.O. Box 8031
Little Rock, AR 72203

Mr. Rick Elumbaugh
Mayor of Batesville
Municipal Building
500 East Main Street
Batesville, AR 72501

Head Librarian
Independence County Library
368 East Main Street
Batesville, AR 72501

Ms. Margaret Harney
Environmental Coordinator
U.S. Fish and Wildlife Service
110 S. Amity Road, Suite 300
Conway, AR 72032

Honorable Bill Hicks
Independence County Judge
Independence County Courthouse
192 East Main Street
Batesville, AR 72501

Mr. Michael P. Jansky
U.S. Environmental Protection Agency, Region 6
1445 Ross Avenue
Suite 1200
Dallas, TX 75202

Ms. Frances McSwain
Deputy State Historic Preservation Officer
Arkansas Historic Preservation Program
1500 Tower Building, 323 Center Street
Little Rock, AR 72201

Ms. Cindy Osborne
Data Manager/Environmental Review Coordinator
Arkansas Natural Heritage Comission
1500 Tower Building, 323 Center Street
Little Rock, AR 72201

Mr. Thomas Rheaume
Branch Manager
Air Division
Arkansas Deparment of Environmental Quality
5301 Northshore Drive
North Little Rock, AR 72118-5317

Mr. Scott Sutterfield
Historic Research Assistant
Arkansas Historic Preservation Program
1500 Tower Building, 323 Center Street
Little Rock, AR 72201

U.S. Fish and Wildlife Service
Arkansas Field Office
110 S. Amity Road
Suite 300
Conway, AR 72032

Mr. Glen Willis
OEM Coordinator
Independence County Office of Emergency Services
192 East Main Street
Batesville, AR 72501

Ms. Penny J. Wilson
Compliance
Hazardous Waste Division
Arkansas Department of Environmental Quality
5301 Northshore Drive
North Little Rock, AR 72118-5317

Electric Drive Vehicle Battery and
Component Manufacturing Initiative Project
FutureFuel Chemical Company, Batesville, AR

DOE/EA-1760
Environmental Assessment
August 2010

This page intentionally left blank.

Appendix A

Agency Consultation

This page intentionally left blank.

The Department of
Arkansas Heritage

Mike Beebe
Governor

Cathie Matthews
Director

Arkansas Arts Council

Arkansas Natural Heritage
Commission

Delta Cultural Center

Historic Arkansas Museum

Mosaic Templars
Cultural Center

Old State House Museum

Arkansas Historic
Preservation Program

1500 Tower Building
323 Center Street
Little Rock, AR 72201
(501) 324-9880
fax: (501) 324-9184
tdd: (501) 324-9811
e-mail:
info@arkansaspreservation.org
website:
www.arkansaspreservation.com

An Equal Opportunity Employer

May 4, 2010

Mrs. Pierina Fayish
U.S. Department of Energy
National Energy Technology Laboratory
Post Office Box 10940
Mailstop B922/M217
Pittsburgh, Pennsylvania 15236

RE: Independence County - Batesville
      Section 106 Review - DOE
      Expansion of FutureFuel Manufacturing Plant
      AHPP Tracking No: 72276

Dear Mrs. Fayish:

This letter is written in response to your inquiry regarding properties of architectural, historical, or archeological significance in the area of the referenced project. My staff has reviewed the documentation regarding the above-referenced undertaking. Our records show that four archeological sites (3IN74, 3IN75, 3IN76 and 3IN77) are located on the subject property and may be affected by the proposed undertaking. These sites were identified in 1974 prior to the initial development of the area. Test excavations at these sites revealed the archeological deposits to be restricted to the surface or the disturbed plowzone. On the basis of the report of that work, we judge these sites to be ineligible for inclusion in the National Register of Historic Places. All four sites subsequently have been heavily damaged or destroyed by construction activities.

Therefore, we have no objection to this undertaking and find that it will have no effect on historic properties. Thank you for the opportunity to comment on this undertaking. If you have any questions, please contact Steve Imhoff of my staff at (501) 324-9880.

Sincerely,

Frances McSwain
Deputy State Historic Preservation Officer

cc: Dr. Ann M. Early, Arkansas Archeological Survey
      Dr. Andrea A. Hunter, Osage Nation
      Ms. Carrie V. Wilson, Quapaw Tribe of Oklahoma

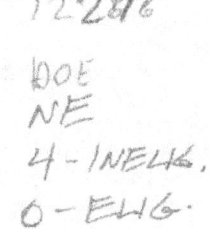

U.S. DEPARTMENT OF
ENERGY

72296
DOE
NE
4 - INELG.
O - EWG.

April 21, 2010

Scott Sutterfield
Historic Research Assistant
Arkansas Historic Preservation Program
1500 Tower Building, 323 Center Street
Little Rock, Arkansas 72201

SUBJECT: U.S. Department of Energy Consultation: Section 106 Compliance for proposed expansion of the FutureFuel manufacturing plant, Batesville, Independence County, Arkansas.

Dear Mr. Sutterfield:

AHPP

The U.S. Department of Energy (DOE) is proposing to provide a financial assistance grant to FutureFuel Chemical Company (FutureFuel), in response to a competitive solicitation funded through the American Reinvestment and Recovery Act (ARRA, or Recovery Act). If approved, the funding would be used to design, install, and operate a commercial-scale plant to produce Intermediate Anode Powder – the key component ConocoPhillip's (COP) line of CPreme® Anode Materials. CPreme® Anode Material is currently qualified in two electric vehicle (EDV) platforms. In order to meet growing product demand and maintain domestic manufacture, COP has entered into an exclusive agreement for FutureFuel to establish full commercial-scale production of Intermediate Anode Powder, with the capability to efficiently expand capacity to meet anticipated market requirements for EDV applications.

An existing FutureFuel manufacturing plant in Batesville, Arkansas, would be retrofitted to process the Intermediate Anode Material. Design of the plant would be based on patented technology and proprietary manufacturing processing methods developed by COP. Construction of additional manufacturing building floor space would not be required for the completion of the project. Site utility systems have adequate capacity to supply the requirements for all phases of the projected plant. FutureFuel also proposes to construct a warehouse and loading docks for the manufactured material, as well as a xylene tank for chemical storage. No significant ground disturbance of undisturbed soils is anticipated.

In addition to this project description, please find attached a USGS 7.5 minute section of the USGS 7.5 minute Salado quadrangle with the project location shown, as well as an aerial map showing the project location.

A search of both National and State historic registers did not reveal any historic structures or sites within the vicinity of the project area.

The Area of Potential Effect (APE) for archaeological resources is defined as the construction impact area. It is unlikely archaeological resources are present within the

APE since the area has been previously disturbed. Furthermore, the plant would be located within existing buildings that will be retrofitted. The character of the project area is industrial.

The APE for architectural resources is defined as being approximately a 1/2-mile perimeter beyond the project limits. The total area of the APE is expected to decrease as the project plans are refined. Project plans are not yet available for this undertaking. There are no known structures within the project APE for architectural resources over 50 years of age.

DOE's initial analysis of the proposed project site indicates that no historic properties are within one-mile of this location, and no tribal lands occur nearby. Therefore, no impacts to historic or cultural properties are anticipated. Since there are no historic resources within the APE for either archeological or architectural resources, DOE has made a finding of No Historic Properties Effected for this undertaking. DOE asks for your concurrence with this finding. Please see the supporting documents attached to this letter for further details on this project.

DOE's National Energy Technology Laboratory is currently preparing an environmental assessment for this proposed project to meet the requirements of the National Environmental Policy Act (NEPA), Council on Environmental Quality regulations (40 CFR 1500-1508), and DOE's NEPA implementing procedures (10 CFR 1021). A copy of the draft environmental assessment will be sent to your office when it is released for a 15-day public comment period. DOE intends to utilize a 15-day public comment period to help facilitate an aggressive schedule for this proposed project and enable the Department to help meet the goals of the Recovery Act.

To aid in the completion of the NEPA process for this proposed project, and to meet DOE's obligations under Section 106 of the National Historic Preservation Act to account for the effects of undertakings by federal agencies on historic properties, DOE is requesting any additional information your office has developed or obtained on historic properties that may occur within one mile of the proposed project site. Please review the attachments which provide the information required for your review. Due to our aggressive schedule, and commitments to implementing the Recovery Act, DOE plans to move forward with the NEPA process for this proposed project. If you cannot provide a response within 30 days of this letter, DOE will continue to the next step as specified in 36 CFR 800.3(c)(4).

Please reply to my attention at the following address:

Mrs. Pierina Fayish
U.S. Department of Energy
National Energy Technology Laboratory
P.O. Box 10940
Mailstop B922/M217
Pittsburgh, PA 15236

I can also be reached at (412) 386-5428 or pierina.fayish@netl.doe.gov.

Sincerely,

Pierina N. Fayish

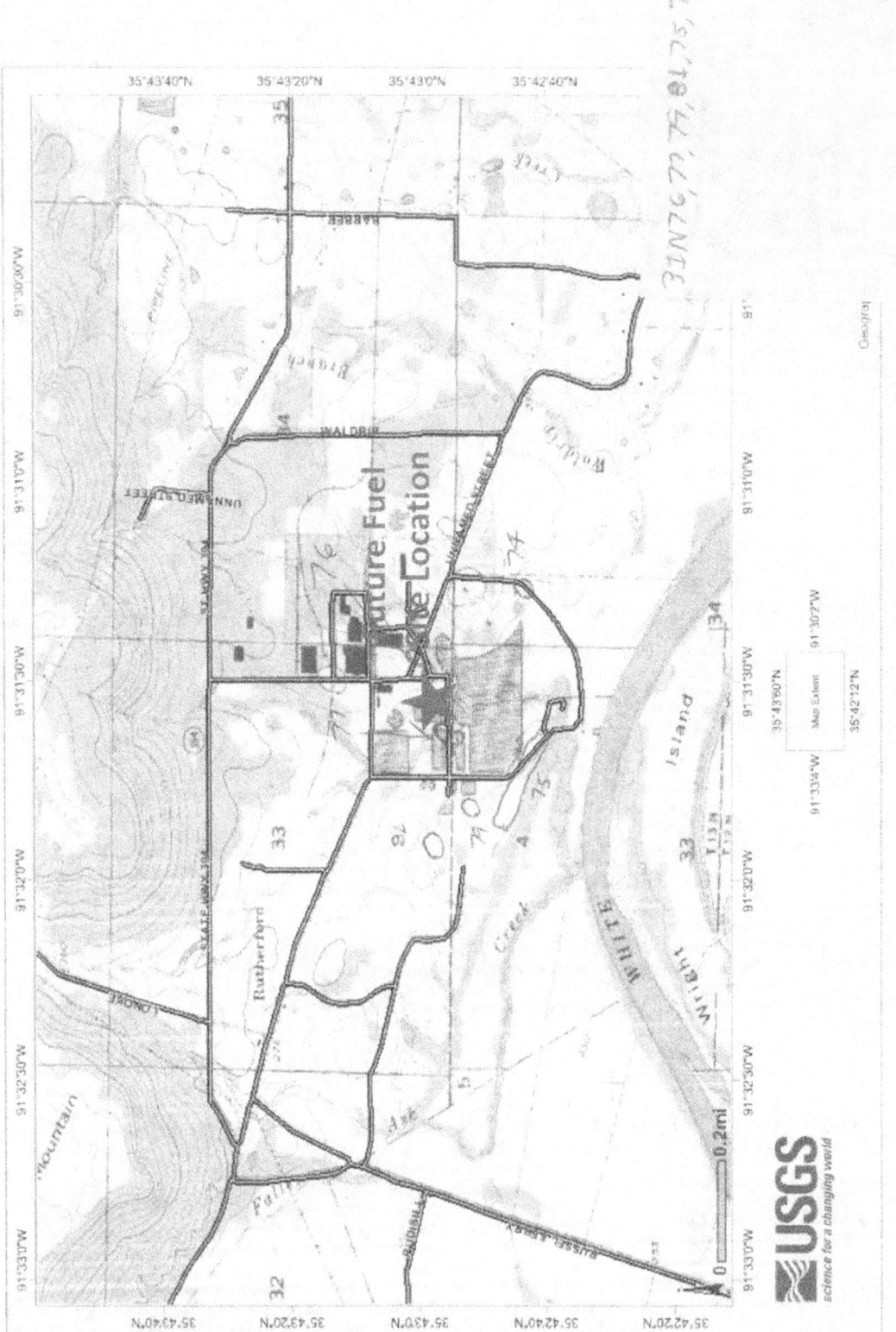

Future Fuel Project Site Topographic Map

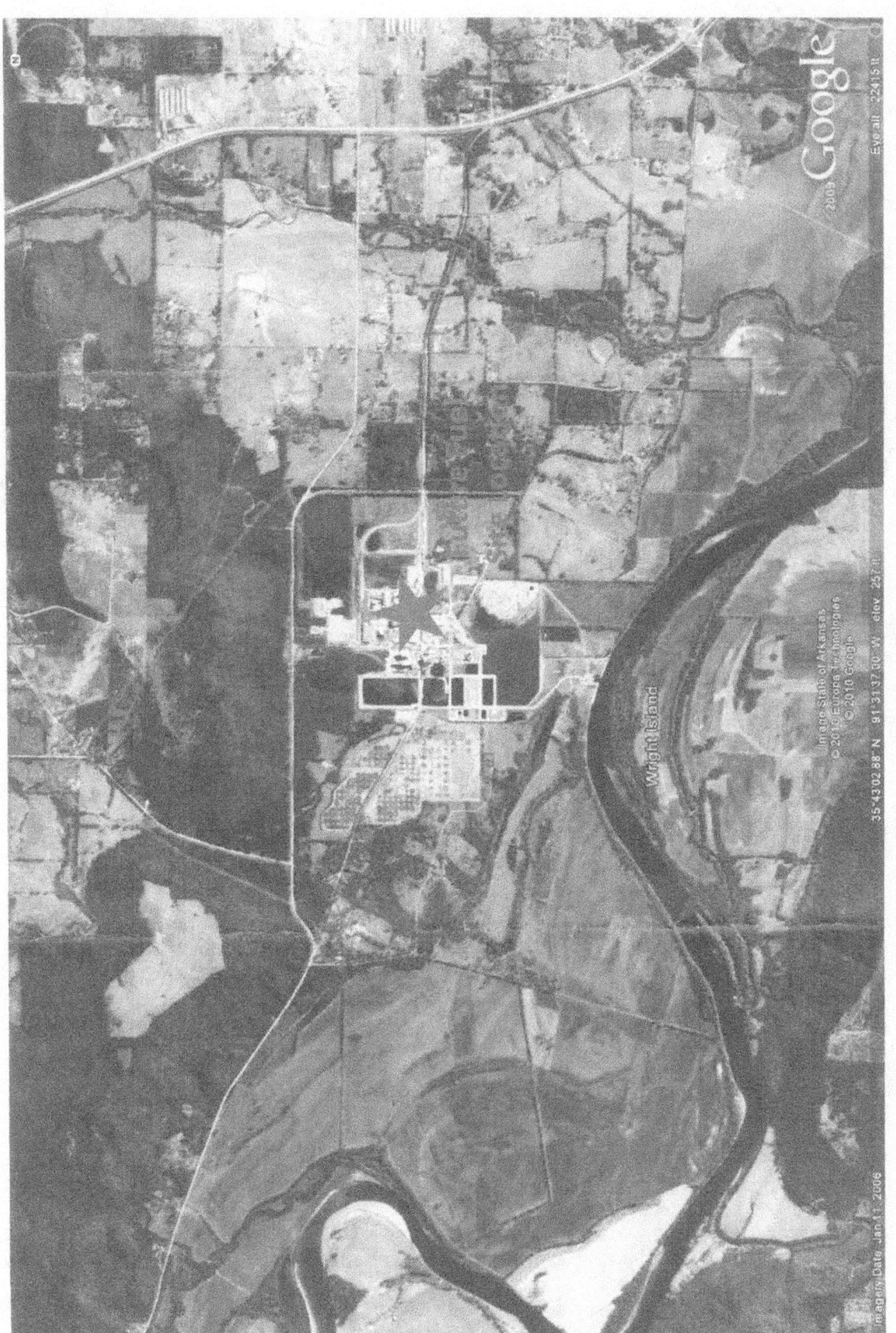

Future Fuel Site Location, Batesville, Arkansas

THE DEPARTMENT OF ARKANSAS

HERITAGE

Mike Beebe
Governor

Cathie Matthews
Director

Arkansas Arts Council

*

Arkansas Historic
Preservation Program

*

Delta Cultural Center

*

Mosaic Templars
Cultural Center

*

Old State House Museum

*

Historic Arkansas Museum

Arkansas Natural Heritage
Commission
1500 Tower Building
323 Center Street
Little Rock, AR 72201
(501) 324-9619
fax: (501) 324-9618
tdd: (501) 324-9811
e-mail:
arkansas@naturalheritage..com
website:
www.naturalheritage.com
An Equal Opportunity Employer

Date: April 16, 2010
Subject: Elements of Special Concern
Commercial Insdustrial Plant (FutureFuel Chemical)
Independence Co., AR
ANHC No.: F-DOE.-10-001

Mr. Robert Naumann
Potomac-Hudson Engineering
7830 Old Georgetown Road, Suite 220
Bethesda, MD 20814

Dear Mr. Naumann:

Staff members of the Arkansas Natural Heritage Commission have reviewed our files
for records indicating the occurrence of rare plants and animals, outstanding natural
communities, natural or scenic rivers, or other elements of special concern within or
near the following site:

Project Name	County	Quad. Name	Location
FutureFuel Chemical	Independence	Salado 7.5'	T13N/R5W/S33
			T13N/R5W/S34

We find no records at present time.

An Independence County Element list is enclosed. Represented on this list are
elements for which we have records in our database. The list has been annotated to
indicate those elements known to occur within a one and a five mile radius of the
project site. A legend is enclosed to help you interpret the codes used on this list.

Please keep in mind that the project area may contain important natural features of
which we are unaware. Staff members of the Arkansas Natural Heritage Commission
have not conducted a field survey of the study site. Our review is based on data
available to the program at the time of the request. It should not be regarded as a
final statement on the elements or areas under consideration. Because our files are
updated constantly, you may want to check with us again at a later time.

Thank you for consulting us. It has been a pleasure to work with you on this study.

Sincerely,

Katie Shannon
for

Cindy Osborne
Data Manager/Environmental Review Coordinator

Enclosures: Legend
Independence County Element List (annotated)

LEGEND

STATUS CODES

FEDERAL STATUS CODES

C = Candidate species. The U.S. Fish and Wildlife Service has enough scientific information to warrant proposing this species for listing as endangered or threatened under the Endangered Species Act.

LE = Listed Endangered; the U.S. Fish and Wildlife Service has listed this species as endangered under the Endangered Species Act.

LT = Listed Threatened; the U.S. Fish and Wildlife Service has listed this species as threatened under the Endangered Species Act.

-PD = Proposed for Delisting; the U.S. Fish and Wildlife Service has proposed that this species be removed from the list of Endangered or Threatened Species.

PE = Proposed Endangered; the U.S. Fish and Wildlife Service has proposed this species for listing as endangered.

PT = Proposed Threatened; the U.S. Fish and Wildlife Service has proposed this species for listing as threatened.

T/SA = Threatened (or Endangered) because of similarity of appearance.
E/SA

STATE STATUS CODES

INV = Inventory Element; The Arkansas Natural Heritage Commission is currently conducting active inventory work on these elements. Available data suggests these elements are of conservation concern. These elements may include outstanding examples of Natural Communities, colonial bird nesting sites, outstanding scenic and geologic features as well as plants and animals, which, according to current information, may be rare, peripheral, or of an undetermined status in the state. The ANHC is gathering detailed location information on these elements.

WAT = Watch List Species; The Arkansas Natural Heritage Commission is not conducting active inventory work on these species, however, available information suggests they may be of conservation concern. The ANHC is gathering general information on status and trends of these elements. An "*" indicates the status of the species will be changed to "INV" if the species is verified as occurring in the state (this typically means the agency has received a verified breeding record for the species).

MON = Monitored Species; The Arkansas Natural Heritage Commission is currently monitoring information on these species. These species do not have conservation concerns at present. They may be new species to the state, or species on which additional information is needed. The ANHC is gathering detailed location information on these elememts

SE = State Endangered; the Arkansas Natural Heritage Commission applies this term to native plant taxa which are in danger of being extirpated from the state.

ST = State Threatened; The Arkansas Natural Heritage Commission applies this term to native plant taxa which are believed likely to become endangered in Arkansas in the foreseeable future, based on current inventory information.

DEFINITION OF RANKS
Global Ranks

G1 = Critically imperiled globally. At a very high risk of extinction due to extreme rarity (often 5 or fewer populations), very steep declines, or other factors.

G2 = Imperiled globally. At high risk of extinction due to very restricted range, very few populations (often 20 or fewer), steep declines, or other factors.

G3 = Vulnerable globally. At moderate risk of extinction due to a restricted range, relatively few populations (often 80 or fewer), recent and widespread declines, or other factors.

G4 = Apparently secure globally. Uncommon but not rare; some cause for long-term concern due to declines or other factors.

G5 = Secure globally. Common, widespread and abundant.

GH = Of historical occurrence, possibly extinct globally. Missing; known from only historical occurrences, but still some hope of rediscovery.

GU = Unrankable. Currently unrankable due to lack of information or due to substantially conflicting information about status or trends.

Arkansas Natural Heritage Commission
Department of Arkansas Heritage
Inventory Research Program
Independence County

Scientific Name	Common Name	Federal Status	State Status	Global Rank	State Rank
Animals-Invertebrates					
Alasmidonta viridis	slippershell mussel	-	INV	G4G5	S1
Amnicola cora	Foushee cavesnail	-	INV	G1	S1
Arrhopalites clarus	a springtail	-	INV	G4	S1S2
Caecidotea ancyla	an isopod	-	INV	G3G4	S2
Cambarus setosus	bristly cave crayfish	-	INV	G3	S1
Cicindela hirticollis	beach-dune tiger beetle	-	INV	G5	S2S3
Cyclonaias tuberculata	purple wartyback	-	INV	G5	S3?
Cyprogenia aberti	western fanshell	-	INV	G2G3Q	S2
Epioblasma triquetra	snuffbox	-	INV	G3	S1
Lampsilis abrupta	pink mucket	LE	INV	G2	S2
Lasmigona costata	flutedshell	-	INV	G5	S3
Ligumia recta	black sandshell	-	INV	G5	S2
Lirceus bicuspidatus	an isopod	-	INV	G3Q	S2
✓ Lucanus elephus	giant stag beetle	-	INV	G3G5	S2
Obovaria olivaria	hickorynut	-	INV	G4	S3
Orconectes neglectus chaenodactylus	ringed crayfish	-	INV	G5T3	S2
Pleurobema rubrum	pyramid pigtoe	-	INV	G2G3	S2
Ptychobranchus occidentalis	Ouachita kidneyshell	-	INV	G3G4	S3
Quadrula cylindrica	rabbitsfoot	-	INV	G3G4	S2
Quadrula metanevra	monkeyface	-	INV	G4	S3S4
Venustaconcha pleasii	bleedingtooth mussel	-	INV	G3G4	S3
Villosa lienosa	little spectaclecase	-	INV	G5	S3
Xolotrema occidentale	Arkansas wedge	-	INV	G1	SNR
Animals-Vertebrates					
Ammocrypta clara	western sand darter	-	INV	G3	S2?
Crotaphytus collaris	eastern collared lizard	-	INV	G5	S3
Cryptobranchus alleganiensis bishopi	Ozark Hellbender	C	INV	G3G4T2Q	S2
Crystallaria asprella	crystal darter	-	INV	G3	S2?
Erimystax harryi	Ozark chub	-	INV	G3G4Q	S3S4
Etheostoma fusiforme	swamp darter	-	INV	G5	S2?
Eurycea spelaea	grotto salamander	-	INV	G4	S3
Haliaeetus leucocephalus	Bald Eagle	-	INV	G5	S2B,S4N
Hiodon alosoides	goldeye	-	INV	G5	S2?
Moxostoma anisurum	silver redhorse	-	INV	G5	S1?
Moxostoma pisolabrum	pealip redhorse	-	INV	G5	S2?
✓ Myotis grisescens	gray myotis	LE	INV	G3	S2S3
Myotis sodalis	Indiana bat	LE	INV	G2	S1
Notropis ozarcanus	Ozark shiner	-	INV	G3	S2
Notropis sabinae	sabine shiner	-	INV	G4	S2?
Ophisaurus attenuatus attenuatus	western slender glass lizard	-	INV	G5T5	S3
Pantherophis emoryi	Great Plains rat snake	-	INV	G5	S3
Percina nasuta	longnose darter	-	INV	G3	S2
Percina phoxocephala	slenderhead darter	-	INV	G5	S2

Scientific Name	Common Name	Federal Status	State Status	Global Rank	State Rank
Percina uranidea	stargazing darter	-	INV	G3	S3
Plethodon angusticlavius	Ozark zigzag salamander	-	INV	G4	S3
Polyodon spathula	paddlefish	-	INV	G4	S2?
Rana sylvatica	wood frog	-	INV	G5	S3
Regina septemvittata	queen snake	-	INV	G5	S2
Scaphiopus hurterii	Hurter's spadefoot	-	INV	G5	S2

Plants-Vascular

Scientific Name	Common Name	Federal Status	State Status	Global Rank	State Rank
Arabis shortii var. shortii	Short's rockcress	-	INV	G5T5	S1
Asplenium pinnatifidum	lobed spleenwort	-	INV	G4	S3
Cardamine douglassii	purple cress	-	INV	G5	S1
Carex conjuncta	a caric sedge	-	INV	G4G5	S1
Carex davisii	Davis' caric sedge	-	INV	G4	S3
Carex gracillima	graceful caric sedge	-	INV	G5	S1
Carex normalis	a caric sedge	-	INV	G5	S1
Castanea pumila var. ozarkensis	Ozark chinquapin	-	INV	G5T3	S3S4
Ilex verticillata	winterberry holly	-	ST	G5	S2
Leavenworthia uniflora	glade cress	-	INV	G4	S3
Maianthemum stellatum	starry Solomon's seal	-	INV	G5	S1
Nemastylis geminiflora	celestial lily	-	INV	G4	S3
Phacelia gilioides	hairy scorpionweed	-	INV	G5	S2S3
Philadelphus hirsutus	mock orange	-	INV	G5	S2S3
Sida elliottii	a sida	-	INV	G4G5	S2S3
Stenanthium gramineum	featherbells	-	INV	G4G5	S3
Stylophorum diphyllum	celandine poppy	-	INV	G5	S3
Trifolium stoloniferum	running buffalo clover	LE	INV	G3	SH
Viola canadensis var. canadensis	Canada violet	-	INV	G5T5	S2

Special Elements-Other

		Federal Status	State Status	Global Rank	State Rank
Colonial nesting site, water birds		-	INV	GNR	SNR
Geological feature		-	INV	GNR	SNR

*-No elements of special concern have been recorded within one mile of the FutureFuel Chemical Company site.

✓-These elements of special concern have been recorded within five miles of the FutureFuel Chemical Company site.

United States Department of the Interior

FISH AND WILDLIFE SERVICE
110 S. Amity Road, Suite 300
Conway, Arkansas 72032
Tel.: 501/513-4470 Fax: 501/513-4480

IN REPLY REFER TO:

May 12, 2010

Reference #: TA0551

Pierina Fayish
U.S. Department of Energy
National Energy Technology Laboratory
PO Box 10940
Mailstop B922/M218
Pittsburgh, PA 15236

Dear Ms. Fayish:

The U.S. Fish and Wildlife Service (Service) has reviewed the information supplied in your letter dated March 29, 2010, regarding proposed retrofitting of the existing manufacturing plant in Rutherford, Independence County, Arkansas. Our comments are submitted in accordance with the Endangered Species Act (87 Stat. 884, as amended 16 U.S.C. 1531 et seq.).

The following endangered species are known to occur in Independence County: Gray bat (*Myotis grisescens*), Indiana bat (*Myotis sodalis*), Pink mucket (*Lampsilis abrupta*), and Running buffalo clover (*Trifolium stoloniferum*). However, the Service has determined that the proposed project is not likely to adversely affect these listed species, as long as there is adherence to the following recommendations.

The true extent of underground environments are difficult to delineate and features such as caves, sinkholes, springs, losing streams, and underground passages may occur on or near your project site, even in previously developed areas. Therefore, the Service recommends the following precautionary measures to avoid impacts to groundwater and sensitive/endangered species not previously known. These include:

1.   Survey for karst features including caves, springs, sinkholes, and losing streams prior to initiating project activities. If such a feature is found, please establish a 300 foot conservation zone around its location and contact the Service for an onsite karst evaluation.

2.   If caves are encountered during construction activities, the Service requests that work efforts cease within 300 feet of the opening. The opening should be adequately marked, fill material should not be placed in the cave, personnel shouldn't enter the cave, and the Service should be contacted immediately.

Best management practices (BMPs) should be properly installed and maintained throughout construction to minimize erosion. These BMPs should be maintained until the site is adequately re-vegetated to prevent soil loss and sedimentation in nearby streams.

Sediment mobilization is the primary concern during construction. However, stormwater runoff following project completion may contain oil/grease, sealants, tar, brake dust, herbicides, pesticides, and additional sediment. To reduce threats to surface and groundwater from these contaminants, the Service recommends the use of detention basins in conjunction with a 100 foot bioswale outfall prior to release in adjacent stream corridors, to manage the first 1" of rainfall events. However, other stormwater management methods including separation systems are available and would be considered if documentation of successful use is provided to the Service prior to installation.

We appreciate your interest in the conservation of endangered species. If you have any questions, please call David Kampwerth at (501) 513-4477 or Stephanie Nelson at (501) 513-4487.

Sincerely,

Margaret Harney
Environmental Coordinator

Appendix B

Public Comments on the Draft Environmental Assessment and Responses from the Department of Energy

This page intentionally left blank.

ADEQ

A R K A N S A S
Department of Environmental Quality

July 23, 2010

William Gwilliam
NEPA Document Manager
National Energy Technology Laboratory
P.O. Box 880
Morgantown, WV 26507

Re: Notice of Availability for Environmental Assessment (EA) for FutureFuel Chemical
        Company, Electric Drive Vehicle Battery and Component manufacturing Initiative
        Project in Batesville, Arkansas

Dear Mr. Gwilliam:

This is in reference to your 7/17/2010 submittal regarding the Independence County –
commercial scale retrofit of an existing structure owned and operated by FutureFuel Chemicals
in Batesville, Arkansas for the manufacture of electric drive vehicle battery and components.
Based upon the information submitted, it appears that the proposed project is environmentally
sound and in compliance with State and Federal laws.

Additionally, if the construction site will disturb in excess of one (1) acre, the permittee must
comply with the terms of the Stormwater Construction General Permit ARR150000 prior to the
start of construction. Please know that any changes to wastewater discharge permitted under
NPDES Discharge Permit AR0035386, due to any circumstances instigated by the proposed
construction, will require a permit modification.

This letter is issued in reliance upon the statements and representations made in the submittal and
the Department has no responsibility for adequacy or proper functioning of the proposed existing
structure retrofit.

If there are further questions, please contact me at (501) 682-0616.

Sincerely,

Mo Shafii
Assistant Chief, Water Division

MS:sw

United States Department of the Interior

FISH AND WILDLIFE SERVICE
110 South Amity Road, Suite 300
Conway, Arkansas 72032
Tel.: 501/513-4470 Fax: 501/513-4480

July 28, 2010

Mr. William Gwilliam
NEPA Document Manager
National Energy Technology Laboratory
3610 Collins Ferry Road
P.O. Box 880
Morgantown, WV 26507

Dear Mr. Gwilliam:

The Fish and Wildlife Service (Service) has reviewed your letter dated July 17, 2010, and Biological Assessment (BA), for the proposed Future Fuel Chemical Company, Electric Drive Vehicle Battery and Component Manufacturing Initiative Project in Batesville, Independence County, Arkansas. Our comments are submitted in accordance with the Fish and Wildlife Coordination Act (FWCA; 16 U.S.C. 661-667e) and the Endangered Species Act of 1973 (87 Stat. 884, as amended 16 U.S.C. 1531 et seq.).

The Service has determined that the proposed retrofit of an existing manufacturing building would not adversely impact any endangered or threatened species nor any non-listed species. We have no further comments.

We appreciate the opportunity to provide these comments.

Sincerely,

Margaret Harney
Margaret Harney
Environmental Coordinator

The Department of
Arkansas Heritage

Mike Beebe
Governor

Cathie Matthews
Director

Arkansas Arts Council

·

Arkansas Natural Heritage
Commission

·

Delta Cultural Center

·

Historic Arkansas Museum

·

Mosaic Templars
Cultural Center

·

Old State House Museum

Arkansas Historic Preservation Program

1500 Tower Building
323 Center Street
Little Rock, AR 72201
(501) 324-9880
fax: (501) 324-9184
tdd: (501) 324-9811
e-mail:
info@arkansaspreservation.org
website:
www.arkansaspreservation.com

An Equal Opportunity Employer

August 2, 2010

Mr. William Gwilliam
NEPA Document Manager
U.S. Department of Energy
National Energy Technology Laboratory
Post Office Box 880
Morgantown, West Virginia 26507-0880

RE: Independence County - Batesville
         Section 106 Review - DOE
         Expansion of FutureFuel Manufacturing Plant
         AHPP Tracking No: 72276

Dear Mr. Gwilliam:

This letter is written in response to your inquiry regarding properties of architectural, historical, or archeological significance in the area of the referenced project. My staff has reviewed the draft Environmental Assessment regarding the above-referenced undertaking. On May 5, 2010, we found that this undertaking would have no effect on historic properties and no new information has come to light that would warrant a change in that assessment.

Thank you for the opportunity to comment on this undertaking. If you have any questions, please contact Steve Imhoff of my staff at (501) 324-9880.

Sincerely,

Frances McSwain

Frances McSwain
Deputy State Historic Preservation Officer

cc: Dr. Ann M. Early, Arkansas Archeological Survey
         Dr. Andrea A. Hunter, Osage Nation
         Ms. Carrie V. Wilson, Quapaw Tribe of Oklahoma

Comment Number	Commenter	Public Comments on FutureFuel EA	DOE Response
1	Arkansas Department of Environmental Quality (ADEQ)	Based upon the information submitted, it appears that the proposed project is environmentally sound and in compliance with State and Federal laws.	Comment noted.
2	ADEQ	Additionally, if the construction site will disturb in excess of one (1) acre, the permittee must comply with the terms of the Stormwater Construction General Permit ARR150000 prior to the start of construction.	As described in Section 2.2 of the EA document, the project primarily involves retrofitting an existing facility; the two proposed ASTs and nitrogen air separator unit package plant combined would result in disturbance to less than 1 acre. Any change to the project which would result in site disturbance in excess of 1 acre would comply with the terms of the Stormwater Construction General Permit ARR150000 prior to the start of construction

The following text is included in the FONSI: "*Additionally, site disturbance resulting from construction would be less than 1 acre. Any change to the project which would result in site disturbance in excess of 1 acre would comply with the terms of the Stormwater Construction General Permit ARR150000 prior to the start of construction*". |
| 3 | ADEQ | Please know that any changes to wastewater discharge permitted under NPDES Discharge Permit AR0035386, due to any circumstances instigated by the proposed construction, will require a permit. | As stated in Section 3.2.2.2 of the EA document current NPDES Permit AR0035386 discharge limits would apply; no modification would be required as chemical composition and thermal characteristics would remain similar to existing discharges permitted. FutureFuel would continue to adhere to the general, monitoring, and reporting requirements contained within the existing NPDES Permit AR0035386. FutureFuel would request a permit modification if changes to wastewater discharged under this permit would occur. |

Comment Number	Commenter	Public Comments on FutureFuel EA	DOE Response
			The following text is included the FONSI: "*No changes to FutureFuel's existing National Pollution Discharge Elimination System (NPDES) Permit are anticipated; FutureFuel, however, would request a permit modification if changes to wastewater discharges would occur.*"
4	USFWS	The Service has determined that the proposed retrofit of an existing manufacturing building would not adversely impact any endangered or threatened species nor any non-listed species.	Comment noted.
5	Department of Arkansas	On May 5, 2010, we found that this undertaking would have no effect on historic properties and no new information has come to light that would warrant a change in the assessment.	Comment noted.

www.ingramcontent.com/pod-product-compliance
Lightning Source LLC
Chambersburg PA
CBHW081221170526
45165CB00009B/2898